THE APOCALYPSE OF ST JOHN

I—III

THE APOCALYPSE OF ST JOHN

I—III

THE GREEK TEXT

WITH

INTRODUCTION, COMMENTARY, AND
ADDITIONAL NOTES

BY THE LATE

F. J. A. HORT, D.D., D.C.L., LL.D.

SOMETIME HULSEAN PROFESSOR AND LADY MARGARET'S READER IN DIVINITY
IN THE UNIVERSITY OF CAMBRIDGE

Wipf & Stock
PUBLISHERS
Eugene, Oregon

Wipf and Stock Publishers
199 W 8th Ave, Suite 3
Eugene, OR 97401

The Apocalypse of St. John I - III
The Greek Text with Introduction, Commentary, and Additional Notes
By Hort, F. J. A.
ISBN: 1-59752-455-7
Publication date 12/5/2005
Previously published by Macmillan, 1908

PREFACE

I CONSIDER it an honour and a privilege to be invited to bear any part in furthering the publication of a work of Dr Hort's; and in the present case the privilege seems to become also a duty. I am aware that there is a feeling abroad, which is general in its character but not without particular application, that injury is done to the reputation of the great men who are gone by publishing works, and still more fragments of works, which they had themselves in no sense prepared for publication. The feeling is natural enough; and it is doubtless true that there are not many scholars who would bear to have such a test applied to them. But Dr Hort was just one of these few; and if the devotion of his friends and the public spirit of his publisher move them to incur the labour and expense of giving such fragments to the world, it is incumbent upon those who benefit by their action to do what in them lies to obtain for it a just appreciation.

It is worth pointing out that the "reputation" which is supposed to suffer is that somewhat vague tribute which the world at large bestows upon the memories of those of whom it has perhaps known little during their lifetime. It is very natural that this tribute should be based—and based by conscious preference—upon finished work,

"Things done, that took the eye and had the price."

But the working student is able to go behind this; and it is the working student whose interest is consulted in such publications as those of which I am speaking, and who is called upon to show his gratitude for them. It is the working student to whom Dr Hort specially appealed as the very *princeps* of his order. What he owes to him is not only an immense mass of really trustworthy data for his own studies, but a model—an unsurpassed model—for the method in which his studies ought to be conducted. Dr Hort was an " expert," if ever there was one. In this respect I should not hesitate to place him first of the three great Cambridge scholars. He had Lightfoot's clearness and soundness of knowledge, with a subtly penetrating quality to which Lightfoot could hardly lay claim; and if Westcott had something of the subtlety, he had not the sharp precision and critical grip. There are grades of excellence in the way in which a scholar handles his evidence. To the average man evidence is like Peter Bell's primrose :

" A primrose by a river's brim
A yellow primrose was to him,
And it was nothing more."

In the case of Dr Hort, each bit of evidence as he comes to it seems to have a life and an atmosphere of its own; and this life and atmosphere is compelled to yield up its secret just as much as the material evidence. In addition to this Dr Hort had a powerful judgement; but I am not quite sure that the judgement was equal in degree to this peculiar faculty of which I have been speaking; it was perhaps biased a little in the opposite direction to that in which most of us have our judgement biased, against the obvious and commonplace. Just this last reason made it of special value as corrective and educative.

Under these heads I am not sure that I know any example of Dr Hort's work that is more instructive than the fragment before us. It is no doubt scholarship in undress—utterly in undress, but perhaps on that account all the more impressive. It is all absolutely bare and severe; there is not a word of surplusage. One seems to see the living scholar actually at work; his mind moving calmly and deliberately from point to point, testing each as it comes up by the finest tests available and recording the results by a system of measurements equally fine. To understand the patience, thoroughness and searching quality of such judgements, is to understand what the highest scholarship really means.

I am not in the secrets of those who have seen through the press the long series of posthumous books with so much loving care, and I do not know on what principle their choice of precedence has been based. Probably it had reference to the degree of preparedness in which the material was left by the author. With a single very small exception—the little volume *Ante-Nicene Fathers*, in which however there are a few sentences scattered through it that I value highly—I should fully endorse their decision to publish. We could not afford to lose the dry light and careful circumspect method of *Judaistic Christianity* and *The Christian Ecclesia*. But in positive value for the student I should be inclined to place first of all the exegetical fragment on I. St Peter, and the present fragment very near it. For criticism as distinct from exegesis, and for the insight that it gives into the workings of a scholar's mind, I doubt if the present fragment can be placed second to anything.

It is true that, as I have said above, the pages that follow were in no sense prepared for the press by their author. Those who know his fastidious judgement might well believe that he had no immediate or near intention of publishing them. And yet they had the advantage of a somewhat thorough revision. I am given to understand that the volume represents notes of lectures delivered first in Emmanuel College in 1879 and then revised for a course of Professor's Lectures in the May Term 1889. Attention may be invited to these dates and to the prescience of coming questions which they seem to indicate; e.g. to the remarkable care which is shown in every allusion to the beginnings of systematic persecution, and the anticipation of the discussions about the early death of St John which a well-known tract by E. Schwartz brought into prominence some fifteen years later. But for the conclusion to which the argument tends we might well think that we were at the standpoint of the present day.

And that conclusion suggests just one more remark before I close. Will not this powerful statement of an old position compel us to reconsider the verdict to which the present generation of scholars appears to be tending? It fell to me a short time ago to review a group of recent works on the Apocalypse (*Journ. of Theol. Studies*, July, 1907), when I summed up on the whole in favour of the current view, though not without considerable reservations. Now, with Dr Hort's fragment in print before me, I cannot help feeling that these reserves are formidably strengthened. In particular the old impression of which I have never been able entirely to rid myself resumes its force, that the historic background as Dr Hort so impressively paints it does suit the Apocalypse better than that of the time of Domitian. Can we not conceive the Apocalypse rising out of the whirling chaos of the years 68–69 A.D., when the solid fabric of the Empire may well have seemed to be really breaking up, more easily than at any other period? And would not the supposition that it did so rise simplify the whole historical situation of the last five and thirty years of the first century as nothing else could simplify it? We could then believe that St John too was really involved in the Neronian persecution—Dr Hort prefers the view that he was banished by the proconsul of Asia, but at least the evidence for banishment by the emperor and from Rome is better, and it would account for the vividness and force of his language where Rome is its subject. We could believe that he escaped barely with his life and by what looked almost like a miracle (the boiling oil, which appears to rest upon what may be a good Roman tradition). We could believe that the experience of these days fired his imagination as Rome in some way evidently had fired it. We could then, under these conditions but hardly under any other, suppose that the same hand wrote the Apocalypse and twenty years or so later the Gospel and Epistles. It is all very tempting, and more coherent than any other solution that is offered to us. And yet we cannot disguise from ourselves the difficulties, as Dr Hort did not for a moment disguise them. It would mean throwing over Irenaeus, and perhaps also Papias, at least to the extent of supposing mistake or confusion. It would mean a less easy interpretation of Rev. xvii. 10, 11, and it may be of vi. 6. It is a choice of evils, and a choice also of attractions. All we can say is that of such puzzles the history, especially of obscure periods, is made.

However this may be, and whatever the ultimate conclusion at which we arrive, I feel sure that students at least will welcome the gift that is now presented to them—if not for its results yet for its method, which has upon it the stamp of a great scholar, individual and incommunicable.

W. SANDAY.

Oxford,
22 *March*, 1908.

NOTE

THE Introduction and Commentary and the former Additional Note were set up in the first instance from the somewhat complicated ms. of Dr Hort's lectures by the skilful printers of the Cambridge University Press. References were then verified and occasionally revised, and abbreviated sentences completed where it seemed necessary. The second Additional Note is added to illustrate Dr Hort's reference on p. xxxii. A few sentences enclosed in square brackets have been introduced from the notes of Dr Murray and others who attended the course in 1889. The Bishop of Ely and Dr Barnes kindly lent their note-books for this purpose. At Dr Murray's invitation I have seen the work through the press; but this has been done only under his constant and kindly supervision.

P. H. L. BRERETON.

St Augustine's College,
    Canterbury.

CONTENTS

APOCALYPSE I—III.

INTRODUCTION.

THREE things most desirable to know about an ancient writing, *Author*, *Readers*, and *Time*.

In many cases the Readers are of little consequence: but not so where their circumstances have evidently determined much of what is said. In this case the Readers are clearly defined: and what there is to be said about them may be deferred for the present.

But the *Author* and the *Time* are matters of warm controversy, and to a great extent the two subjects are mixed up together, though, on one side at least, there is no necessary connexion.

As a starting-point we may take the traditional view, which contains in itself several statements. "John, the son of Zebedee, the author of the Gospel and Epistles bearing his name, wrote also the Apocalypse in the reign of Domitian." Since the Apocalypse was certainly due to persecution, and no persecution of Christians in Domitian's reign is known except at its very end, the date must on this view be 95 or 96, as he was killed in September, 96.

Now at the outset it should be observed that no part of this composite statement can appeal to the *direct and express* testimony of the N.T. Of course the words "direct and express" are everything. But neither the Gospel nor the Epistles contain within themselves the name of their author: the titles are no part of them. The Apocalypse does claim to be written by a John, but does not say what John. Lastly it neither names Domitian nor gives any clear reference to circumstances of his reign. That on all these points the N.T. does contain important evidence cannot be doubted. But it has to be elicited by critical processes. It does not lie on the surface, so that all may read.

The peculiar character of the Apocalypse has at various times called forth vague doubts about its authorship.

Genuine criticism in a true historical spirit on this subject belongs to centuries XVIII and XIX, but especially to the last 50 years. It has of course dealt with both problems, *time* and *authorship*.

(1) *As to Time.*

There has been an endeavour to ascertain internal evidence of time.

The starting-point has been that change of view respecting prophecy which is part of the general change of view about the Bible altogether. The essential feature in this change is the recognition of human agency as the instrumentality by which the Spirit of God works.

In prophecy this implies a recognition, as regards recipients, of their present circumstances and needs; so that a practical purpose is never absent in prophecy. As regards the prophet himself, it implies a recognition of his own perception of the inner forces under the outward events of his time, as also of his perception of God's permanent purposes as the foundation of his prophetic vision; so that the Divine inspiration does not supplant the workings of his own mind, but strengthens and vivifies them.

This is rather general language. The special force of it for critical purposes consists in the attempt to discern in a prophetic book what particular horizon of circumstances and events was before the prophet's mind.

Now in the Apocalypse the general tendency of criticism has been towards the view that the circumstances and events present to the writer's eye are not those of Domitian's time, and are those of the time between Nero's persecution (about 64) and the fall of Jerusalem (70), *i.e.* at least 25 years earlier than on the common view.

As we shall see, the question of authorship may have to contribute additional evidence. But thus far the question of date is independent of authorship.

(2) *As to, Author.*

Criticism here has been set in motion by the literary problem of the relation of the Apocalypse to the Gospel and Epistles.

The dissimilarity lies on the surface, being most marked in the style of Greek, but extending also to words and ideas, some of the most characteristic phrases of the Gospel being evidently absent from the Apocalypse.

Thus for a long time past it has appeared to many self-evident that the two books had different authors. On this assumption two different theories have been built.

The earlier critical school of the present century, including many illustrious names, felt the enormous difficulty of believing any one but one of the original Apostles to have written the Gospel, while they saw no such difficulty as regards the Apocalypse. They therefore attributed it to another John, mostly to the Presbyter John mentioned in early times. This view is still widely held by competent and sober critics.

It has, however, been greatly shaken by the later critical school originating at Tübingen, who have seized on the other alternative. They refuse to believe the Apostle to have written the Gospel; they think it quite likely that he should write the Apocalypse, which they represent as full of a narrow Jewish spirit, and they point to the undoubtedly very strong external ancient evidence for the authorship of the Apocalypse by the Apostle.

Within the last few years a small knot of critics has gone further still, rejecting the Apostle as the writer of either book. This last view rests on very slender and precarious grounds, and I do not propose to say much about it, as it would be impossible in the time to discuss every possible theory.

The critical dilemma has much more claim to consideration. If the difficulty of attributing both books to the same author were found really insuperable, I believe it would then be right to hold some other John to be the author of the Apocalypse, and such a view is quite compatible with reverence for the book as a part of the N.T., as in the case of the Epistle to the Hebrews.

But the *positive* side of each contending view is very strong, chiefly internal evidence for the Gospel, chiefly external evidence for the Apocalypse: and the apparent force of the dissimilitude is much lessened if the earlier date of the Apocalypse is the true one.

The difference is not of years merely but of the whole aspect of events. The fall of Jerusalem and extinction of the Jewish State, in combination with the long years spent away from Palestine in a great Greek city, are, I believe, enough to account for the unlikeness.

Thus it seems to me that criticism has shewn the traditional view to be wrong as to date, but not as to authorship, while without the correction as to date the authorship would be very perplexing.

It was, I think, the son of Zebedee who wrote both books, but the Apocalypse many years before the Gospel.

The Unity of the Book.

Thus far we have been considering the problem of the date and the authorship of the Apocalypse on the assumption which till lately was practically made on all hands, viz., that the book had but one author, and was written at one time. As however some of you are doubtless aware, this assumption can no longer be treated as agreed to on all hands. More than once, indeed, in earlier times it had been suggested by commentators of real mark that the Apocalypse was really a combination of elements of different authorship and date ; but the suggestion had practically fallen into abeyance till seven years ago, when it was revived by Dr Völter, a *Privatdozent* or lecturer at Tübingen. What however gave a more powerful impulse in the same direction was the essay of a young Giessen student, Eberhard Vischer, which was taken up and published with a commendatory epilogue three years ago by Harnack, who is a deservedly high authority on Church History, less so I think on biblical probléms. The special idea contributed by Vischer was that our Apocalypse consists of an early Jewish Apocalypse, to which at a later time a Christian had added a beginning and end, with various retouchings and small interpolations throughout. The idea was less original than it seemed. (1) It has long been a favourite idea with some Continental writers, an entirely mistaken one, I believe, that the record of our Lord's own apocalyptic discourse in the first three Gospels includes a kernel or core transcribed from a purely Jewish Apocalypse. (2) Harnack himself has of late done good service by shewing how greatly the extent and importance of Jewish Christianity had been exaggerated ; and in so doing he has been in too great a hurry to cut knots by assuming Christian interpolations of Jewish writings. (3) The historian Theodore Mommsen, in the fifth volume of his *Roman History* (520 ff.), published four years ago, had stigmatised the anti-Roman language of the Apocalypse as due to Jewish bitterness. And (4) Völter's tract had raised anew the question as to the possible compositeness of the Apocalypse. Thus Vischer's theory grew naturally out of the joint effect of various antecedents. The same causes which led to its existence have contributed also to making it plausible and acceptable to many readers ; and accordingly it has met with assent to an extent that is not a little startling. Moreover it has called forth various hypotheses differing from it to a greater or less extent, but dominated by the same idea. One of the latest is set forth in an elaborate book of nearly 600 pages, in which Vischer's position is inverted (as indeed had already been done by French critics): here the Apocalypse is described as a Christian book, redacted and enlarged by a Christian editor with additions partly his own, partly Jewish.

It would of course be impossible for me here to enter on the intricate controversies raised by these various theories. The whole term would not suffice for even an imperfect examination of them. It must suffice to say that, so far as I am acquainted with them, they have done nothing whatever to shake the traditional unity of authorship. It is a subject which ought to be approached entirely without prejudice, as regards either the theories or their authors. The problem is a critical one, and must be discussed on critical grounds. Those who wish to see a good statement of the case on behalf of the unity of the book, and can read German, will find it in an admirable article in the *St. u. Kr.* for 1888, No. 1, by Professor Beyschlag, a competent and open-minded critic. No doubt it was written before much of the now existing literature had appeared : but its arguments have full force with respect to the whole subject, not merely to accidental details of individual criticism. The bearing of this question on the subject of this term's lectures is indirect only, viz., as affecting the question of date. No one, I believe, doubts that the first three chapters are Christian, not Jewish. The most important fields of controversy are chapters xi., xii., and some of the later chapters. These first three chapters do indeed contain some of the most important passages for determining the kind of Christianity held by the Christian or Christians who wrote the book or part of it; and these we shall naturally have to examine. But I have called attention to the subject to-day, partly because its interest (I trust, its temporary interest only) requires it, but chiefly because the unity of the book is presupposed in what I have to say about its date and authorship.

After this general sketch of the problems of date and authorship, and the results which on the whole seem to be best established, we must now examine the evidence rather more carefully.

Evidence as to Time.

We begin with evidence for Domitian's reign. This is virtually external only, but the testimony is undoubtedly weighty.

The first and most serious is that of Irenaeus in last quarter of second century. Justin before 150 had mentioned the book as by the Apostle John, but said nothing about date.

Irenaeus (v. 30), referring to the number of the Beast, says that "if it had been necessary that his name should be publicly proclaimed at the present season, it would have been uttered by him who saw the Apocalypse. For it was seen no such long time ago, but almost in our own generation, at the end of the reign of Domitian (σχεδὸν ἐπὶ τῆς ἡμετέρας γενεᾶς, πρὸς τῷ τέλει τῆς Δομετιανοῦ ἀρχῆς)." Irenaeus also mentions in two places (ii. 22 ; iii. 3) that John survived till the reign of Trajan. Irenaeus was himself a native of Asia Minor; he was a hearer of Polycarp of Smyrna, who was a personal disciple of St John ; and he used the treatise of Papias of Hierapolis, another personal disciple of St John. Thus he had peculiarly good means of knowing the truth.

On the other hand Clement of Alexandria, not much later, in his tract *Quis div. salv.* 42 (p. 949 Potter), tells a story of what befel St John when after the tyrant's death he had passed from the island of Patmos to Ephesus (ἐπειδὴ γὰρ τοῦ τυράννου τελευτήσαντος ἀπὸ τῆς Πάτμου τῆς νήσου μετῆλθεν ἐπὶ τὴν Ἐφ.). And Clement's disciple Origen early in the third century, commenting on Matthew xx. 22 f. ("drink the cup...with the baptism," &c.), tom. XVI. 6, says that "the emperor of the Romans, as tradition teaches, condemned John to the isle of Patmos" (ὁ δὲ Ῥωμαίων βασιλεύς, ὡς ἡ παράδοσις διδάσκει, κατεδίκασε τὸν Ἰωάννην μαρτυροῦντα διὰ τὸν τῆς ἀληθείας λόγον εἰς Πάτμον τὴν νῆσον), and further quotes St John (Apoc. i. 9) as referring to his μαρτύριον, but not mentioning who had condemned him. The absence of a name in both Clement and Origen certainly does not prove that no name was known to them. But the coincidence is curious, and on the whole suggests that the Alexandrian tradition assigned the stay in Patmos to banishment by an emperor, but did not name the emperor. The story speaks twice of St John as old (τὸν γέροντα), and implies that his age (ἡλικίας) would be an impediment to him in his running to pursue the flying young man. So far as it goes, this suits Domitian best, but it does not go for much. It is not at all clear that even the journey on which he first saw the young man was meant to be taken as immediately following the return from Patmos, rather than merely in that part of St John's Ephesian stay : also there may have been a considerable interval (χρόνος ἐν μέσῳ) before the second interview: and finally even at the earlier date John was not a young man. Clement's words would be compatible with exile independent of the emperor, provided that the

b 2

emperor's death ended the persecution. But Origen distinctly refers the exile to the emperor's act. Tertullian, the elder contemporary of Clement, speaks (*Ap.* 5) of Domitian, a second Nero in cruelty, as recalling those whom he himself had banished, but does not there mention St John. In *Praesc.* 36, in celebrating the Roman Church and its glories, he refers to the martyrdoms of Peter and Paul, and says that *there* the Apostle John was plunged in fiery oil without suffering anything, and was banished to an island, which seems to imply banishment by the emperor himself. "Si autem Italiae adjaces, habes Romam, etc. Ista quam felix ecclesia cui totam doctrinam apostoli cum sanguine suo profuderunt, ubi Petrus passioni dominicae adaequatur, ubi Paulus Johannis exitu coronatur, ubi apostolus Johannes, posteaquam in oleum igneum demersus nihil passus est, in insulam relegatur."

The story of the burning oil (Porta Latina), which plays a large part in later legend (Ps.-Prochorus), recurs in the Latin Abdias, *Apost. Hist.*, v. 2 (Fabr. ii. 534 f.), but it is referred to Ephesus, and made the act of the Proconsul, who, on the Apostle's emerging safe, desires to release him, but fearing the edict of the emperor (*Domitian*) banishes him to Patmos by way of a milder punishment.

Either Rome locally, or the act of the Roman emperor, must be meant when Hippolytus (*De Chr. et Antich.* 36) apostrophises John calling upon him to speak of Babylon, καὶ γὰρ αὕτη σε ἐξώρισεν.

Next perhaps Victorinus of Petavio, in Pannonia, if he is the author of some Latin notes on the Apocalypse. He died about the beginning of the fourth century. The notes at all events distinctly say that John was condemned by Domitian to the mines in Patmos. To the same effect Primasius ("a Domitiano Caesare exilio missus et metallo damnatus"). Then comes the historian Eusebius, who simply states (iii. 18) that in the reign of Domitian St John was condemned to inhabit the isle of Patmos, and then quotes Irenaeus. Further on (iii. 20. 9) he tells us that according to the tradition of the ancients (ὁ τῶν παρ' ἡμῖν ἀρχαίων παραδίδωσι λόγος) John, under Nerva, the successor of Domitian, returned to Ephesus from his banishment in the island. Finally (iii. 23) for the late date to which St John lived he quotes the two passages of Irenaeus on Trajan and also the passage of Clem. Alex., the latter apparently as shewing that St John at least survived the exile to Patmos.

In another book (*D. E.* iii. 5, p. 116 c) he groups in a single sentence Peter's crucifixion at Rome, Paul's beheading, and John's banishment to an island; it is not quite certain that he meant Rome to have been the scene of the third event as well as the first two, but probably he did. Καὶ Πέτρος δὲ ἐπὶ Ῥώμης κατὰ κεφαλῆς σταυροῦται, Παῦλός τε ἀποτέμνεται, Ἰωάννης τε νήσῳ παραδίδοται.

After Eusebius comes Jerome who always largely follows him. In his *V. I.* 9 he says that "persecutionem movente Domitiano [in his fourteenth year] in Patmos insulam relegatus scripsit Apocalypsim"; but that when Domitian was slain, and his acts on account of their excessive cruelty had been rescinded by the Senate, he returned to Ephesus under Nerva. All this from Eusebius. Again writing against Jovin. i. 26 (280 A), he says that John saw the Apocalypse in Patmos, to which he had been banished by Domitian, and then goes on to say that Tertullian reports about the burning oil. A singular passage intended to shew the superiority of the unmarried apostle St John to the married apostle St Peter: "Sed Petrus apostolus tantum, Joannes et apostolus et evangelista et propheta.... propheta, vidit enim in Pathmos insula, in qua fuerat a Domitiano principe ob Domini martyrium relegatus, Apocalypsim infinita futurorum mysteria continentem. Refert autem Tertullianus quod Romae [a Nerone] missus in ferventis olei dolium purior et vegetior exiverit quam intraverit." (Curious that for "*Romae*" Vallarsi says that all the MSS. (et vetus editio) read "*a Nerone*"; and perhaps they are right, for there is no reason why Jerome should not have supposed this to be a previous incident though mentioned second; and though Tertullian says nothing about Nero, Jerome may have unconsciously inscribed the name from tradition.) He again refers, without naming Tertullian, but only "ecclesiasticas historias," to the story in his Commentary on Matthew xx. 23, 155 f. In both these places (see Lipsius i. 419 f.) the accompanying language suggests that Jerome had some knowledge of a legendary narrative akin to what we find extant later.

Contemporary with Jerome, about 375, was Epiphanius, a careless and confused writer, but deeply read in early Christian literature, to whom we owe the preservation of much valuable information from ancient times. His treatise on heresies has a long article on the Alogi, gainsayers of both the Gospel of St John and the Apocalypse, which there is good reason to believe to have been partly founded on a lost treatise of Hippolytus. Twice in this article Epiphanius uses peculiar language. First (li. 12, p. 434 A), John refusing in his humility to write a Gospel (εὐαγγελίσασθαι) was compelled by the Holy Spirit to do so, in his old age, when he was 90, after his return from Patmos, which took place under Claudius Caesar. After many years of his sojourn in Asia he was compelled to publish the Gospel. Again (33, p. 456 A) the Apocalypse is referred to for a prophecy uttered by the mouth of John before his death, he having prophesied in the times of Claudius Caesar, and yet earlier, when he was in the isle of Patmos. The first passage allows, or rather requires, a considerable interval (ἱκανὰ ἔτη) between the Apocalypse and the Gospel; while the second, referring to the Apocalypse alone, by the way in which Epiphanius uses the phrase "before his death" (πρὸ κοιμήσεως αὐτοῦ), suggests lateness of the book, which would involve the supposition that Epiphanius supposed Claudius to have been emperor in John's extreme old age. This seems hardly credible, and it is more likely that the language in the second place is merely slipshod. But the reference to Claudius remains in both places, and must have come in some shape from some earlier authority, whether Hippolytus or not. The emperor whom we call Claudius died in 54, ten years before the persecution of Nero. A banishment of St John at that time is incredible, and it is not likely that he was the emperor really meant. But as one of his names was Nero, so also our Nero was likewise a Claudius, and is often called on inscriptions Nero Claudius or Nero Claudius Caesar. It seems probable therefore that, whatever Epiphanius may have meant, his authority meant and perhaps said Nero.

Later writers generally follow Eusebius and Jerome. They were the most learned men of the fourth century, and the nature of their books made them standards for facts of history.

There are however some curious deviations from the common tradition. The Syriac version of the Apocalypse of unknown date says that *Nero Caesar* had banished John to Patmos. The Apocryphal Acts of John the Son of Zebedee, edited by Wright from the Syriac (p. 55), tell that "Nero, the unclean and impure and wicked king, heard all that had happened at Ephesus; . . . and he laid hold of St John and drove him into exile." Then follows the vision of an angel to Nero, who induces him to send and fetch John back to Ephesus; and (57) "the word of Nero was established over his own place, but he did not dare again to give orders regarding the province of Asia; it was this wicked man who slew Paul and Peter."

There are also in commentators both Greek and Latin signs of an interpretation that referred various verses to the Fall of Jerusalem. If it were quite certain that the words were taken to be predictive, this would be inconsistent with the Domitian date. But it is conceivable that these interpretators took St John as speaking of what was passed (cf. Areth. ap. Cramer Cat. viii. p. 282, 5 f.). So Andreas *Comm. in Apoc.* 19 (on vii. 1), εἰ καὶ ταῦτά τισιν ὑπὸ Ῥωμαίων πάλαι τοῖς Ἰουδαίοις γεγενῆσθαι, ἐξείληπται,...πολλῷ μᾶλλον τοῦτο ἐν τῇ τοῦ Ἀντιχρίστου ἐπελεύσει γενήσεται. Cf. Andreas on vii. 3, 4. Arethas, *Comm. in Apoc.* 19, refers vii. 1, 4, 8 to the Fall of Jerusalem. "Tichonius" *Exposit. in Apoc.* 13 (see Migne August. *op.* iii. App.), commenting on xvi. 14, "Potest hoc loco dies magnus intelligi illa desolatio, quando a Tito et Vespasiano obsessa est Ierosolyma."

To recapitulate. We find Domitian and Nero both mentioned, as also an emperor not named. The matter is complicated by the manner in which St John is brought to Rome, or his banishment referred to the personal act of the emperor. It is moreover peculiarly difficult to determine the relation of the legend of the boiling oil to the Roman tradition of a banishment from Rome.

On the one hand the tradition as to Domitian is not unanimous; on the other it is the prevalent tradition, and it goes back to an author likely to be the recipient of a true tradition on the matter, who moreover connects it neither with Rome nor with an emperor's personal act. If external evidence alone could decide, there would be a clear preponderance for Domitian.

Another argument for the late date is the fact that an epistle is addressed to Laodicea, and none to Hierapolis and Colossae, its neighbours in the valley of the Lycus (cf. Col. iv. 13). It is urged that acc. to Tac. *Ann.* xiv. 27 Laodicea was ruined by an earthquake in 60, and its restoration is mentioned; also Eus. *Chron.* 64 or 5 mentions all three towns as ruined by an earthquake. The contention is that Hierapolis and Colossae were probably not rebuilt for many years afterwards, and therefore are ignored by St John. But this is most precarious. Laodicea is apparently singled out because it restored itself without Roman help (nullo a nobis remedio propriis opibus revaluit), a very unusual thing. Earthquakes were very frequent thereabouts, and rebuilding doubtless followed at once. Cf. Lightf. *Col.* pp. 3, 38 ff. St John doubtless names Laodicea alone, as being the most important, and representing the three.

The remaining argument urged for his time may be stated in Alford's words (p. 233): "We have no evidence that the first or Neronic persecution extended beyond Rome, or found vent in condemnations to exile; whereas in regard to the second (Domitian's) we know that both these were the case." This is however an imperfect statement. St John's exile at Patmos is only a part of what we learn from the Apocalypse on this matter, and the smallest part. His banishment, if such it was, is nothing to the terrors and miseries out of which the book proceeds. It is emphatically the book of martyrdom of the N.T. The cry of the souls of the slaughtered under the altar (vi. 9 f.), "How long, O Master, the holy and true, dost thou not judge and avenge our blood of them that dwell on the earth?" is the undertone throughout. It is perhaps not safe to dwell much on the martyrdom of Antipas at Pergamum (ii. 13), which is distinctly mentioned, for this was perhaps not quite recent, and perhaps due to local incidents. But persecution must have been lying heavy on churches which filled a large part of St John's horizon and apparently on the churches of Asia to which he wrote. If it had not reached them, it was evidently close at hand: moreover Rome must have been felt as a deadly antagonist.

Now in enquiring whether these conditions apply best to the days of Domitian or to the earlier period we are constrained to recognise how little we really know about either persecution. Of a persecution in *Asia Minor* at either time we know absolutely nothing except from the Apocalypse itself.

Known[1] *Evidence of Domitian's Persecution.*

Tacitus lost. Suetonius silent as to the name at least, though he mentions the Neronian persecution; [and therefore his short anecdotal manner does not account for omission of a persecution of Christians, were it of importance.]

D. Cassius lost in his integrity. His abbreviator Xiphilinus (lxvii. 14) tells how at the end of his reign Domitian killed ($\kappa a\tau \acute{\epsilon}\sigma\phi a\xi\epsilon v$) (among many others) Flavius Clemens, a man of consular dignity, a cousin of his own, and married to Flavia Domitilla, a kinswoman of his own. Both were charged with atheism ($\mathring{a}\theta\epsilon\acute{o}\tau\eta\tau os$), by which ($\mathring{v}\phi$' $\mathring{\eta}s$) many others also diverging to Jewish customs were condemned. And some died and others were deprived of their property, and Domitilla was merely banished to Pandateria. He then goes on, apparently in the same connexion, to speak of the murder of Glabrio, who had been Consul with Trajan. Again, in the beginning of the next book (lxviii. 1), among the acts of Nerva reversing the odious deeds of Domitian, it is said that "he released those that were under trial for impiety ($\mathring{a}\sigma\epsilon\beta\epsilon\acute{\iota}q$), and restored the banished; and put to death all slaves and freedmen who had conspired against their masters. And such persons he allowed to bring no other charge against their masters, and other persons he allowed to accuse no one either of impiety or of Jewish life."

---

[1] See Lightfoot, *Clem. Rom.* i. p. 104 ff.

The actual incident of the death of Flavius Clemens is noticed by Suetonius (15) as the last of Domitian's crimes, and what especially hastened his fall. He calls Flavius Clemens, Domitian's cousin, a man "contemptissimae inertiae," whose two sons, though yet children, he had publicly designated as his own successors, and says that Domitian put him to death suddenly, on a very slender suspicion, almost in his very consulship. The event is also noticed very briefly by Philostr. (*V. Apoll.* viii. 25) in connexion with a remarkable account of the death of Domitian.

But further, Eusebius in his *Chronicon* states that according to Bruttius, an almost unknown heathen author (cf. Eus. *H. E.* iii. 18. 4), many Christians suffered martyrdom under Domitian (in his 15th year, Eus. *l. c.*). Among them Flavia Domitilla, niece of Flavius Clemens, a consul, was banished to the isle of Pontia because she avowed herself to be a Christian. Syncellus adds, perhaps from the same source, " Clemens himself was put to death for Christ's sake."

To examine the whole story would take too long. Enough to refer to Lightfoot, *Phil.* 22 f., and *Clem. Rom.* i. pp. 33 ff., who shews the groundlessness of the doubts which have been raised as to Flavius Clemens and his wife being Christians, referring especially to De Rossi's discovery of the Coemeterium Domitillae as a Christian burying-place.

There is no historical value in the late acts of martyrdom of Nereus and Achilles professing to belong to this time (see Lightfoot, *Clem.* i. p. 44).

But a very authentic, only unfortunately vague, mention of this persecution is connected with Flavius Clemens, viz. the Epistle of Clement of Rome to the Corinthian Church. All the best critics now agree that it dates from the persecution of Domitian. It begins with saying that the Roman Church had been somewhat slow in offering counsel about the strifes at Corinth " owing to the sudden and rapidly succeeding misfortunes and reverses coming upon us " (διὰ τὰς αἰφνιδίους καὶ ἐπαλλήλους γεινόμενας (so Syr.; Lft.[2] γεν.) ἡμῖν συμφοράς), where ἐπαλλ. of course implies plurality, but still more, quick succession, one treading on the heels of another. The language is not like what would be used if the persecution had been other than local, but there it was evidently at once unexpected and severe. Clement the writer has sometimes been identified with Flavius Clemens the consul, but was doubtless, as Lightfoot shews, a freedman in his service.

Later accounts are vague ; enough to shew that there was a real persecution at Rome, but not more, though doubtless consistent with more.

Melito *ap.* Eus. iv. 26. 9 puts together Nero and Domitian as alone of the emperors having been persuaded by envious men to place our doctrine ἐν διαβολῇ.

Tert. *Ap.* 5 : Reperietis primum Neronem in hanc sectam... ferocisse...Temptaverat et Domitianus, portio Neronis de crudelitate, sed qua et homo, facile coeptum repressit, restitutis etiam quos relegaverat.

This may be compared with the account of Hegesippus in Eus. iii. 20 how Domitian set free the grandsons of Jude arrested as of David's family, and by an edict stopped (κατέπαυσεν) the persecution against the Church, a statement which reminds us of what Tertullian says, and is certainly independent of it.

Lact. *de Mort.* 3 implies only that Domitian's death followed soon.

Sulp. Sev. *Chr.* ii. 31 : Domitianus, Vespasiani filius, persecutus est Christianos. In the next sentence he goes on to St John's banishment to Patmos. But it is curious that in the previous chapter he attributes to Titus, Domitian's brother, the counsel at the taking of Jerusalem that the temple should be destroyed, on the ground that the religion of the Jews and Christians would be more fully abolished (tolleretur), since these religions, though contrary to each other, yet proceeded from the same authors : that the Christians owed their existence to the Jews; and when the root was taken away the stem would easily perish. The passage to which this statement belongs is shewn by Bernays (*ü. d. Chron. d. Sulp. Sev.* 56 ff.) to be almost certainly taken from a lost passage of

Tacitus, who is peculiarly likely to have known the real facts, in opposition to the account of Josephus, written in flattery of Titus. It shews an enmity to Christianity on the part of at least one member of the Flavian family.

Orosius alone (vii. 10) speaks of a widespread persecution, "confirmatissimam toto orbe Christi ecclesiam datis ubique crudelissimae persecutionis edictis convellere auderet." But he is apt to be extravagant and superlative in language, and has no independent authority.

Conclusions with regard to Domitian's Persecution.

The last few months of Domitian's life were a veritable reign of terror, in which many of the noblest Romans were sacrificed. Among them were two near kinsmen of Domitian himself, Flavius Clemens and Domitilla. Their Christianity was evidently brought against them, though it is more probable that this was a mere pretext. But we cannot doubt that other Christians perished too, perhaps many others, whether by the putting in force of a dormant edict of Nero's, if the edict implied in Pliny's letter was his, or by a new edict, or without an edict under comprehensive laws. Yet there is nothing in the accounts which suggests anything like a general persecution of Christians, even at Rome : it would rather seem that Christians of wealth or station were mainly, if not wholly, struck at. And further, the two accounts of Tertullian and Hegesippus leave it difficult to doubt that Domitian himself stopped the persecution. Beyond [the mention by Hegesippus of the arrest of Jude's grandsons and] the vague statement of the late Orosius, there is not a particle of evidence for persecution beyond Rome, and there is nothing in external events as far as they are known to lead either to that or to any great disturbance of society. The special features that seem to fit St John are not really distinctive. What is told of banishment by Domitian would suit the case of St John only if he was banished from Rome, a possibility certainly not to be discarded, considering some of the legends, when our knowledge is so small; but still only one alternative. And even so the coincidence is much less important than it might seem at first sight, for banishment to islands was not peculiar to one reign. See a long list in Mayor on Juv. i. 73.

The returns from banishment spoken of by D. Cassius have probably nothing to do with Christianity. The crime mentioned is *impiety*, which at this time often meant only treason. It is perversely confused by Aubé with ἀθεότης, of which Flavius Clemens was accused. The coincidence is therefore not to be relied on in the absence of correspondence in the general state of things.

Evidence of Nero's Persecution.

A careful and in most respects satisfactory examination in C. Franklin Arnold's tract *Die Neronische Christenverfolgung*, Leipzig, 1888.

Here we have first Tac. *Ann.* xv. 44. The occasion being the burning of Rome in July, 64. To turn aside the suspicion against himself Nero suborned accusers of the Christians. Tacitus calls them "per flagitia invisos," also "sontes et novissima exempla meritos," including them among "cuncta atrocia aut pudenda," and so also he says they were convicted of "hatred of the human race" even more than of setting the city on fire. [Is Tacitus carrying back into Nero's days the ideas of Trajan's time? There is nothing to support this; all the minutiae hold together.]

Suet. *Ner.* 16, without any reference to the fire (cf. 38), among Nero's various public acts, chiefly legislative, includes "afflicti suppliciis Christiani, genus hominum superstitionis novae ac maleficae." It comes between regulations about what might be sold in the cooks' shops and others about restraining the license of charioteers and the factions of clowns.

The event greatly impressed Christians, and Nero stands out preeminent in tradition as the first persecutor. But (apart from traditions about St John, and the earlier story of Pomponia Graecina) the only names or incidents in any way handed down are the martyrdoms of St Peter and St Paul, and those with curious variations. Eusebius has no more to tell us.

Clem. Rom. 5, tells of Peter and Paul, probably though not distinctly, as martyred at Rome, and then speaks of many others as having likewise suffered many torments.

Tert. *ad Nat.* i. 7, "sub Nerone damnatio [nominis hujus] invaluit...quales simus damnator ipse demonstravit, utique aemula sibi puniens. et tamen permansit erasis omnibus hoc solum institutum Neronianum justum denique ut dissimile sui auctoris." Yet this does not say much ; especially when compared with *Apol.* 5, "dedicatore damnationis nostrae" (nothing more specific). On the other hand Sulp. Sev. *Chr.* ii. 29, "Hoc initio (Nero) in Christianos saeviri coeptum : *post etiam datis legibus* religio vetabatur, *palamque edictis propositis* Christianum esse non licebat."

With regard to the edict, at all events it would be rash to build much upon it.

Hence here, too, we have very little material for testing the appropriateness of the Apocalypse.

Grounds for asserting the Neronian date.

But two points seem decisive :

(1) The whole language about Rome and the empire, Babylon and the Beast, fits the last days of Nero and the time immediately following, and does not fit the short local reign of terror under Domitian. Nero affected the imagination of the world as Domitian, as far as we know, never did. On some evidence of this there is more to be said just now. [Note the combination of Nero and the populace. This is characteristic of the adverse power in Apoc.]

(2) The book breathes the atmosphere of a time of wild commotion. To Jews and to Christians such a time might seem to have in part begun from the breaking out of the Jewish war in the summer of 66. Two summers later Nero committed suicide, and then followed more than a year of utter confusion till the accession of Vespasian, and one long year more brings us to the Fall of Jerusalem. To the whole Roman world the year of confusion, if not the early months of Vespasian's reign, must have seemed wholly a time of weltering chaos. For nearly a century the empire had

seemed to bestow on civilised mankind at least a settled peace, whatever else it might take away. The order of the empire was the strongest and stablest thing presented to the minds and imaginations of men. But now at last it had become suddenly broken up, and the earth seemed to reel beneath men's feet. Under Vespasian, however, the old stability seemed to return : it lasted on practically for above a century more. Nothing at all corresponding to the tumultuous days after Nero is known in Domitian's reign, or the time which followed it. Domitian's proscriptions of Roman nobles, and Roman philosophers, and Roman Christians, were not connected with any general upheaval of society. It is only in the anarchy of the earlier time that we can recognise a state of things that will account for the tone of the Apocalypse.

It is therefore to no purpose that critic after critic protests that we have no evidence of the persecution of Nero having extended beyond Rome. This is quite true,—if we leave the Apocalypse out of sight, but it applies equally to the persecution of Domitian. The question really is (1) whether the Apocalypse is intelligible if there was no persecution of Christians except that local and apparently short persecution described by Tacitus ; and (2) which of the two persecutions was most likely to call forth terrible echoes of itself in other lands. The absence of evidence doubtless comes from the absence of all Christian records for this period.

I do not wish to occupy time with commenting on the correspondence between Pliny and Trajan. But I am very thankful now to be able to refer to Lightfoot (*Ign.* I. 7—17) as shewing that it is wholly wrong either to treat Trajan as first introducing important persecution, or to suppose that previously the Christians were habitually confounded with the Jews by heathens, and therefore shared their immunities in the earlier period. Whether Christians were by name forbidden to exist, or condemned under more general laws, condemnation was assuredly always a danger which they had to fear : and there is no reason why this state of things should not date from the time of Nero.

It may be added that several verses seem to refer to the deaths of SS. Peter and Paul; chiefly called prophets, once (xviii. 20) apostles and prophets, as in Ephesians[1]. So (cf. xvi. 6, not clearly Rome) xvii. 6; xviii. 24; xix. 2 (besides xviii. 20): and though this language might be used at the later time, it acquires special force if the deaths were still recent, and the Church were still in the midst of the sore trial of which their deaths were an early stage.

These grounds are sufficient [for placing Apoc. perhaps in the earliest months of Vespasian's reign]. Though not resting much on single definite facts, they are strong on a broad view.

Besides them other grounds are given of a more definite kind, regarded by some critics as quite decisive. So indeed they would be if the interpretation of the passages on which they depend were certain. I have not however been able to satisfy myself enough as to the interpretation to be able to lay much stress on them. They are interesting in themselves: and I could not with propriety pass them over.

They are:

I. *The relations between the seven heads of the Beast* (xvii. 9 ff.; cf. 7, 8; xiii. 2).

v. 9 leaves no doubt that in some sense John has Rome in view, the seven hills. Whatever the relation of the heads, mountains, and kingdoms may be (not at all clear), it is certainly said that five kings are fallen, one is, the other is not yet come, and when he shall come, he must abide a little while. This is supposed to be a summary of imperial history. The five are Augustus, Tiberius, Gaius, Claudius, Nero. A difference of opinion as to the present emperor, some urging Galba, the first of the three emperors of the anarchy; others Vespasian, the first emperor after the anarchy. Whatever may be the truth of these interpretations, the positive objections commonly made to them are frivolous. To begin counting the emperors from Augustus rather than Julius is the more correct reckoning of the two: and the treatment of the anarchy as a mere interval is fairly justified by such language as Suet. *Vesp.* 1, "Rebellione trium principum et caede incertum diu et quasi vagum

[1] ii. 20; iii. 5. See *Christian Eccles.* p. 165.

imperium suscepit firmavitque tandem gens Flavia." When it is
said of apparently the same Beast (xiii. 2) that one of his heads
was as it were stricken to death, and that the death wound was
healed, this is referred to the blow received by the empire by the
anarchy on Nero's death, and its gradual recovery to order. So
again much is written on the words in xvii. 8, how the Beast "was
and is not," which are similarly interpreted.

II.   *The future Head as the returning Nero.*

The words about the future or seventh king, who is also
apparently eighth, and also of the seven (xvii. 10 f.) are referred
either to an expected return of Nero or to Domitian as a new
embodiment of the spirit of Nero. Certainly at the beginning of
Vespasian's reign Domitian, who first represented him at Rome,
bore a hateful character : "Omnem vim dominationis tam licenter
exercuit ut jam tum qualis futurus esset ostenderet" (Suet. *Dom.* 1).
One suggestion that has been made by Weiss (*St. u. Kr.* 1869,
pp. 49 f.) should be noticed. If Domitian in his youth, not yet
emperor, was regarded as the future head of the beast, he would in
a very true sense be a main subject of the Apocalypse, and the best
coming representative of the hostile forces against which St John
represented the Church as contending : and it is conceivable that if
this were known and remembered, the association of his name with
the book might by a possible confusion, after Domitian had come to
be known as a persecutor, pass into a tradition that the book was
written in his reign.

But the most striking feature of the times in connexion with
this interpretation is the supposed connexion of this language of
St John with popular belief in the return of Nero[1]. This is the
most telling element in Renan's melodramatic picture ; but he has
to resort to large exaggerations. Still the facts are impressive
enough. First, Nero had won a kind of popularity; nay by the court
which he had paid to the mob, by the exhibition of games, by his

---

[1] See Haakh in Pauly *Encyclop. d. Class. Alt.* v. 584 f.

crimes, and his whole wild personality, he had deeply impressed the minds of many by a kind of demoniacal influence. "There were not wanting," says Suet. 57, "men to adorn his tomb with spring flowers and summer flowers for a long period," and his name was held in a strange kind of veneration. Presently rumours arose that he was not dead, but would soon return to take vengeance on his foes. Several pretenders to the name did actually appear at different times. Dio Chrysostom, who died about 117, says (*Or.* xxi. p. 271) that "even now all desire him to live: nay most men think he does, although in a sense he has died not once but many times along with those who supposed him to live." But, as Weiss shews, the belief was not in a resurrection, but simply in his being hidden away in the East, not having really died. The widely spread modern notion that there was a contemporary expectation of his mysteriously returning from the dead rests on a confusion between the ideas of different times. Nero, we must always remember, died young, not yet 32. If, therefore, the popular notion that he was not dead, but a fugitive in the East, had been true, there would have been nothing unreasonable for the next 40 or 50 years in looking for his return from the East; and that period carries us down later than the latest conceivable date of the Apocalypse. It was not till the full three score years and ten or four score years had elapsed from his birth, that the expectation of his reappearance could put on that supernatural character which is implied when the language of the Apocalypse is accounted for in this way.

Both the earlier and the later representations find a place in the miscellaneous collection of poems of different ages called the Sibylline Oracles, as has been well shewn by Zahn in his *Apok. Stud.* in Luthardt's *Zeits. für k. Wissen. und k. Leben* for 1886; but the two can be clearly distinguished, and it is apparently in one of the later portions that we first encounter the idea of a Nero who is practically Antichrist, as distinguished from the great wicked king, the matricide, fleeing beyond the Euphrates, and coming back with uplifted sword and many hosts. In the Christian Apocryphon, *Ascensio Esaiae* iv. 2, Berial appears with characteristics borrowed from Nero; "there shall descend Berial, a mighty angel, king of this world,...under the appearance of a man, an impious king, the murderer of his own mother, even the king of this world"; but no personal appearance of Nero is intended. From these relatively late Sibylline Oracles the idea of a Nero-Antichrist (or forerunner of Antichrist) passed into some Latin writers of the West, as the poet Commodian, and probably the commentator, Victorinus of Pettau, and thus gained a place which it long held in Latin tradition. But the late origin of this conception of Nero destroys its supposed value as fixing the date of the Apocalypse by means of that single passage of xvii; while on the other hand all the language of the Apocalypse suggested by the Roman Empire has its full force only if it was written when the terrible spell of Nero's career was freshest in its power over the imagination of mankind.

III. The number of the Beast (xiii. 18).

If this riddle could be certainly read, it might tell much. Two solutions only deserve mention, ΛΑΤΕΙΝΟϹ (in Irenaeus), which might in a manner suit the Roman Empire at any time, but never well, and at all events is not distinctive. Of late years, however, much has been said on the Hebrew *Neron Kesar*. The absence of the Yod is nothing: there is excellent authority for that. There are, however, two strong difficulties: (1) despite the Hebraising of the book, it is strange that a book written in Greek to men who probably did not know a word of Hebrew should need Hebrew for the solution: and (2) whatever importance the image of Nero may have as the personal representative of the Roman Empire, it is not his own personal name that we should look for as given to the Beast. To identify the two is to confuse the parts.

IV. The measuring of the city (xi. 1 ff.).

It is often assumed that this refers to the anticipated fall of Jerusalem, either from the siege having actually begun or because events were so tending towards it that it could be clearly anticipated, more especially in the light of our Lord's own words (*e.g.* Lk. xxi. 24, probably founded on Zech. xii. 3, LXX.). That some sort of reference to the actual siege, known or anticipated, is here, is certain. But there are great difficulties in taking the whole passage as referring to definite external events. The distinction between the shrine and the outer court is better understood, as by Weiss and Gebhardt, of the outer shell of rejected Israel, and the true inner Israel, the Church of Jesus Christ, the only genuine representation of the old holy people (cf. i. 6). It is urged indeed by Düsterdieck that, whatever the precise interpretation, there is a reference to the treading down as in the future, and this is true, and yet not quite conclusive. If a spiritual separation is intended, it is just conceivable that the prophet might use the material treading down, which was already past, as a suggestive symbol for the future. This however is not likely, and the example of Ezekiel does not help, because there the whole point lay in the future restoration of the temple. Here then, as in some of the other evidence, the earlier date is not absolutely enforced, but it alone is natural; and so far this point of the allusions to the temple might stand as well among the positive evidence as to date.

Thus, to gather up the result of the whole, the evidence alleged by recent critics for the early date on the ground of sharp and absolutely decisive personal details seems too uncertain, in respect of St John's meaning, to be relied on at present with full assurance. But on the other hand the general historical bearings of the book are those of the early, and are not those of the late period. The force of Irenaeus's testimony cannot be denied: it is a real difficulty, because on this matter his information was likely to be good[1]. But it is on the other hand true that, supposing *no* tradition to have come down from the Apostolic age, and it to be known, as we see it was from independent places of Irenaeus, that St John had lived till Trajan's reign, it was very natural to put the banishment of i. 9 into the last preceding known persecution. Probably it was a mere guess, like the later guess, that Domitian himself banished him,

[1] But see Appendix on Bovon, *Rev. de Théol. et Philos.*, July 1887 (p. 358 ff.).

and like the analogous guess that Nero, the other great persecutor, was the offender. On the Neronian traditions themselves little stress can be laid. What they do attest is the limited range of the Irenaean tradition.

On the evidence to date dependent on difference of style from the Gospel see pp. xxxvii ff.

Authorship.

I.   Positive external evidence.

II.   Positive internal evidence as to identity with son of Zebedee.

III.   Positive internal evidence as to identity with author of the Fourth Gospel.

I.   External Evidence for St John.

Just. *Dial.* 81, "A certain man among us, whose name was John, *one of the apostles of the Christ*, in a *Revelation* (ἀποκαλύψει) made to him prophesied that they who believed our Christ should pass 1000 years in Jerusalem, and after that the universal and in a word eternal resurrection and judgment of all at once with one accord should come to pass" (Apoc. xx. 4—6).

There are several other instances early or in middle of second century, in which the Apocalypse of John was quoted as authority, but no *direct* evidence that the Evangelist was meant. There is no evidence, however, or indication to the contrary. The names are Papias of Hierapolis, Melito of Sardis, Epistle of Gallican Churches, Muratorian Canon, Theophilus of Antioch. But all these are only fragments, if so much.

When we come to great extant writers of late second and early third centuries, the testimony is clear as to the Evangelist being the author. So Irenaeus, and later Hippolytus; Clement and Origen; Tertullian and Cyprian. To this time, on the other hand, belong Epiphanius' Alogi, *i.e.* those of Hippolytus. They rejected *both the Gospel and Apocalypse,* not the Apocalypse for the sake of keeping the Gospel for John. They ascribed them to Cerinthus. They were probably stimulated by reaction against Montanism, a strongly progressive movement; its doctrine of the Paraclete in the Gospel, of chiliasm in Apocalypse: probably also against the growing doctrine of the Word, and the theology that was being founded upon it.

One other early writer partially agreed with them, the Roman presbyter Gaius. Not long ago there was room for serious doubt as to the identity of the Book of Revelation which he condemned; and his very personality was so shadowy that Dr Lightfoot was able to make out a strong case for identifying him with Hippolytus. However, that is all at an end now. Not many months ago Dr Gwynn of Dublin published extracts from a MS. Syriac Commentary (century XII.) on the Apocalypse containing distinct replies of Hippolytus to distinct objections made by Gaius. These passages prove that Gaius rejected our Apocalypse on the ground of discrepance with the Gospels and with St Paul's Epistles, while there is no sign that he rejected St John's Gospel.

We now come to a peculiar episode in the history of the reception of the book, the line taken by Dionysius of Alexandria. See Eus. vii. 24, 25, esp. the following: "Afterward he speaks in this manner of the Apocalypse of John. 'Some before us have set aside and rejected the book altogether, criticising it chapter by chapter, and pronouncing it without sense or argument, and maintaining that the title is fraudulent. For they say that it is not the work of John, nor is it a revelation, because it is covered thickly and densely by a veil of obscurity. And they affirm that none of the apostles, and none of the saints, nor anyone in the Church is its author, but that Cerinthus who founded the sect which was called after him the Cerinthian, desiring reputable authority for his fiction, prefixed the name'" (vii. 25. 1—2). Cf. iii. 28.

It is difficult to say whether he refers to contemporary gainsayers, or to Alogi, or to yet others. In any case doubtless their opposition was owing to dislike of chiliasm. His own careful criticism is based on internal grounds. He makes no reference to tradition on either side.

Latter part of third century obscure. Methodius certainly names a John as author, "the blessed John" (p. 94 Jahn). "Christ called πρωτ. τ. νεκ. by the prophets and the apostles" (p. 95), and apparently he means John the Evangelist. See also *Conviv.* pp. 13, 28, 30, 35, 44.

Eusebius disturbed (1) by his own hatred of chiliasm, (2) by respect for Dionysius Alex., leaves all undecided, after his manner.

Thenceforward the question is not of authorship but of authority, and a very difficult and ill explored question it is. The Latin Churches, as from the first, thoroughly upheld the book; the Syriac Churches as a rule rejected it. The Egyptian versions omitted it (Lightfoot in Scrivener's *Introd.* 3rd ed. pp. 389, 398). The Greek East was divided: sometimes it occurs in catalogues of Scripture, sometimes not. Now and then shy quotations from it occur: but on the whole it is conventionally accepted and in practice for the most part ignored.

It is startling to glance over an apparatus criticus to the text of the Apocalypse, such as that of Tischendorf, and see how astonishingly few quotations of it are found in Post-Nicene Greek Fathers, except in the two commentators, Andreas, of somewhat uncertain age, and Arethas his follower, who is now clearly fixed to the early years of century x.

But there is no evidence that this state of things in respect of the use practically made of the Apocalypse has any real relation to the question of authorship. Throughout, from first to last, there is no trace whatever of any historical tradition, except of John the Apostle. The dissent comes apparently only from internal criticism on the part of those who disliked its teaching or were puzzled and embarrassed by it. The rasher sort coolly attributed it to Cerinthus, the traditional antagonist of St John; a careful and reverent man like Dionysius of Alexandria hunted about in the N.T. for other Johns. Practically, as far as our knowledge goes, antiquity knows only John the Apostle. But of course in this as in other matters tradition may err: and further evidence is desirable.

No evidence is contained in τ. θεολόγου. The name was probably given to St John the Evangelist in virtue of his Prologue. The first known application of it to him is in Ath. *Or. c. Gent.* 42, ᾗ φησι καὶ ὁ θεολόγος ἀνὴρ Ἐν ἀρχῇ κ.τ.λ. Substantially the same, however, in Eus. *H. E.* iii. 24. 13, that St John omitted the human genealogies, τῆς δὲ θεολογίας ἀπάρξασθαι. And so θεολογέω in century IV., &c., is often used absolutely for calling Christ God (cf. Eus. *H. E.* v. 28. 4 f.), being previously used for calling anyone θεός. Another possible origin of the title is the use of θεολόγος for prophets of God found in Philo *V. Mos.* 311 (ii. 152), *Fr.* (ii. 668) and Methodius *De res.* ii. 6, p. 93. Also Eus. *D.E.* ii. p. 9 [?] (*ap.* Hilg. *Einl.* 407). But apparently the earliest occurrence in the title is in B₂, end of VIII. Not in other uncials or in the title of the Gospel.

II. *Positive Internal Evidence.*

There is very little either way. The reference to "the twelve apostles of the Lamb" in xxi. 14 has been urged against the authorship of the son of Zebedee. The question is simply whether one of the number could so write. It is really difficult to discuss the point seriously. Setting aside the relation to the vision, supposing it were part of John's message to convey this teaching, was he to omit it because he was included in it? or was he to put in some additional words to shew his own relation to the rest? Surely nothing could have been more incongruous and unlikely. This verse then is simply neutral.

So also, I think, is with one exception the whole book. There is nothing in it which specially belongs to one of the twelve, nothing at variance. If it be asked whether we should not expect some positive signs of an apostle, if the writer were one, the very peculiar contents of the book remove any seeming strangeness. The one exception is the tone which St John takes throughout. He does not, it is true, call himself an apostle, but why should he? St Peter's example is virtually solitary (St James and St Jude not being apostles), for St Paul *not* being of the twelve, had need to assert his apostleship.

St John had no such need, and, moreover, he wrote more as prophet than as apostle, not to make known the revelation given in our Lord's life, but the new revelation. But he does write in the tones of conscious authority. It is true, this might be prophetic authority simply: so that this would not be a serious difficulty if a second John, prophet but not apostle, were on other grounds likely. But still the most natural way of understanding the language is to take it as that of one of the chosen Three among the chosen Twelve.

III. *Internal Evidence as to identity with author of Fourth Gospel.*

This is a vast subject, far too vast for more than a few words. As regards difference of language and ideas, there is little to add to what I said before. The differences are great, so great that if the name John were absent, and if both Apocalypse and Gospel came down to us anonymously, difference of authorship would at least occur to us more naturally than identity of authorship. But this is not the problem. This evidence is only a part of the whole: and the question for us is simply whether it be so strong as to over-power the other evidence for identity, and whether there is not other evidence of a contrary kind.

As regards language, the only really important difference is the number of constructions not truly Greek in the Apocalypse, and their absence from the Gospel. These peculiarities are either crude Hebraisms, or such as may easily be explained as phrases of one accustomed to think and speak in Hebrew rather than in Greek. A large proportion might be described simply as relaxations of the laws of concord in appositional phrases, in which there is a re-version (so to speak) from oblique cases to the nominative as the primary case, or from the feminine to the masculine as the primary gender. The best account is in Ewald's Latin *Comm.*, 37—46 (de linguae indole). A good summary also in Credner's *Einl.* 731 f.; a diffuse but not minute one in Lücke *Offenb.* 448 ff. Winer, from his just hatred of finding Hebraisms everywhere, is too little disposed to recognise them in the Apocalypse. Supposing St John to have spent most of his life till then in Palestine (cf. Jos. *Ant.* xx. 11. 2), the phenomena are natural enough. It is not at all likely that he purposely chose this kind of language, though no doubt the nature of the subject made it easier to adopt. But still the fitness is there, and helps us to understand that we are listening to the last of the Hebrew prophets. It would have been just as *un*natural if after 25 and more years of a Greek life he had not learned to write more correct Greek. But it is only the incorrectnesses that vanish. The Gospel of St John (and to a great extent his Epistles), though rarely Hebraistic, is entirely and intensely Hebraic in form as well as substance. Its sentences have no Greek elaboration, they have the broad Hebrew simplicity. The only other book comparable is St James, and there the Hebrew substratum is hidden by distinct Greek culture. It is also striking that the chief exceptions to this simplicity are made by the naked inclusion of one sentence within another without mutual adaptation. Thus Ev. iv. 1 ff.; i. 14—16; x. 12 f.; cf. xiii. 1—4, and Apoc. i. 5 f.; 17 f.; also ii. 2, 9; iii. 8 f.

As regards ideas and words representing them there are again no doubt great differences, but not contradictions, and there are also some striking resemblances. For the two sides see Lücke 662—744, and Gebhardt, *Doctrine of the Apoc.* (last section), who, however, somewhat exaggerates the resemblance. Everyone notices ὁ λόγος τ. θεοῦ (xix. 13) and ὁ λόγος, conceptions in their contexts by no means identical, but the one leading to the other, the Apocalypse standing between the O.T. and the Gospel. Not the least remarkable point is the selection of this name at all in such a context in the Apocalypse. And again iii. 14 ἡ ἀρχὴ τ. κτίσεως τ. θεοῦ carries us back in another way to the Prologue. But the Christology of the Apocalypse is too large a subject to take only in passing. On this and other points of the relation between the two books see Westcott *St John* lxxxiv ff. Two other subordinate but far-reaching connexions I must mention, the peculiar prominence of the idea of μαρτυρία in both books, and (what is often noticed) νικάω [conquering by seeming defeat]. The relation to Judaism we shall have other opportunities for examining in connexion with the passages supposed to be Anti-Pauline. Notice at once the double position, devotion to Israel, yet bitter feeling that it was lost (xi. 1 f., esp. 8). In the Gospel both are there again, but the proportion is changed, the doom being now manifest: yet still it is εἰς τὰ ἴδια and οἱ ἴδιοι; οἱ Ἰουδαῖοι have joined the side of evil, but this is just the misery: it is what only a Jew could feel completely.

What strikes me, however, most strongly in the way of connexion is the sharp opposition of good and evil in concrete forms in the Apocalypse and in the other writings. No other books of the N.T. have anything like it. The opposition of the Holy City, the New Jerusalem, and Babylon is the most salient exhibition of it in the Apocalypse, but, indeed, it runs all through the book. In the Gospel the form is altered: St John has exchanged the Empire and the woman seated on the seven hills for ὁ κόσμος. To anyone who recalls the respectful language of St Paul and St Peter towards the heathen rulers, the recognition of them as having an authority from God and a work to be done for God, it is startling to read the language of the Apocalypse. But it is those last days of Nero that explain the contrast, the days when the supreme power seemed to be only the organ of the vilest passions of the most degraded humanity. In the Gospel we have come back to the serener air of the earlier time, and the more permanent view (as it were) of the relations of Christians to other men. But the antithesis, which in the Apocalypse puts on a peculiar and exceptional form, due to the circumstances of the time, is in itself too fundamental to be absent from the Gospel, though now the antagonist is "the world," for "the world" includes every embodiment of the Babylonian spirit. In the Gospel St John goes back to our Lord's own words, while he also applies them in his own person. Like the elder prophets he had first been led to see a vision of judgment in a concentrated form as it were, all brought into a single picture near at hand; and then learned by degrees that it had to be worked out by a slow process. This antagonism of powers takes various forms: but both Apocalypse and the other Johannine books are pervaded by it.

Thus on the whole I see no sufficient reason in diversity of language or ideas for assigning the Apocalypse to a different author.

Various good critics who have done so have also been so much struck by coincidences of spirit as to say that the author of the Gospel must have been a careful student of the Apocalypse. When we get thus far, it is merely arbitrary to suppose that our criticism can perform with certainty so delicate a task as that of discriminating the relation of a Christian writer to a younger yet very mature disciple from that of a Christian writer between Nero and Vespasian to the same writer in the days of Trajan; they are, to speak roughly, only two different cases of the one relation, "the child the father of the man." If we could find any tolerable evidence for the theory that the author of the Apocalypse was a bigoted Jew, and the author of the Fourth Gospel a subtle philosophising Greek, it would no doubt be hard to imagine the passage from the one into the other. But these representations are baseless fictions, and the real differences of the books need no such violent transition to bridge them over.

It is however true that without the long lapse of time and the change made by the Fall of Jerusalem the transition cannot be accounted for. Thus date and authorship do hang together. It would be easier to believe that the Apocalypse was written by an unknown John than that both books belong alike to St John's extreme old age. The supposition of an early date relieves us however from any such necessity, and the early date is, we have seen, much the most probable on independent grounds.

Circumstances.

The question whether it was through banishment that St John found himself in Patmos turns on the interpretation of i. 9, the discussion of which may stand over for the present [see on i. 2]. No doubt the exile is a tolerably constant feature of the traditions, but in all probability the source of the belief is that verse itself thus interpreted, and cannot be safely relied on as independent evidence. To-day it is enough to say that the familiar interpretation seems to me much the most probable, though just now another interpretation is very popular.

There were two grades of banishment, *deportatio* (περιορισμός) and *relegatio* (ἐξορία). The word used in the traditions of St John is *relego*, but in non-legal writers it sometimes denotes vaguely any kind of banishment. (Rein in Pauly VI. i. 429 *sub fin.*) *Deportatio*, which succeeded to the *aquae et ignis interdictio*, was among the *capitales poenae*, and involved greater loss and degradation than *relegatio*, which might be for either a limited time (half a year to ten years) or for life. See especially *Dig.* xlviii. 19, 28 (Callistratus), also xlviii. 22. The power of deportation was reserved for emperors and the city prefect, that of relegation belonged also to the senate, the praetorian prefect, and the governors of provinces. Unless therefore St John was banished from Rome, he must have suffered the milder *relegatio*. Among the recorded banishments to Aegean islands hardly any are to those on the West coast of Asia Minor, the Cyclades being preferred. This somewhat confirms the supposition that the Proconsul of Asia banished St John. Governors of provinces had the power of relegation to islands belonging to their own province, if it possessed islands: otherwise they could only give sentence in general terms and then write to the emperor to get him to assign an island (*Dig.* xlviii. 22. 7, Ulpian). But there can be little doubt that Patmos (very obscurely mentioned in ancient writers) would belong to Asia: the separate province of the isles is apparently only of much later date.

There is no inherent impossibility of St John's having accompanied St Peter to Rome, and for some special reason having suffered banishment at the hands of Nero; and this would agree with the language of Tertullian, and apparently the Roman tradition. St Peter and St John appear together in John xxi.; Acts iii. 1 ff.; iv. 13 ff.; viii. 14—25. But little as we know about St Peter at Rome, it is not at all likely that if St John had been with him the fact would have escaped notice. This and the choice of Patmos suggest the probability that the banishment was from Asia (*e.g.* Ephesus) and by the proconsul.

The only place in N.T. (excluding Apocalypse) where St John appears in person after the early part of Acts is Gal. ii. 9, with

reference to St Paul's visit to Jerusalem about 51, when St James
the Lord's brother, St Peter and St John agreed with St Paul
and Barnabas that they should take the Gentiles, themselves the
circumcision. We know nothing of the Churches of Judea from
Acts after Acts xi. except so far as they are connected with the
work of St Paul. Neither the time nor the occasion of either his or
St Peter's leaving Jerusalem can be fixed with certainty. Eus. iii.
5. 2, 3 speaks of the martyrdom of St James, and of the rest of the
apostles having had innumerable plots against their lives and being
driven from Judea and setting out to preach the Gospel among all
nations with the power of the Christ, in that He had said to them
"Go ye, &c.," and moreover (οὐ μὴν ἀλλά) of the people of the
Church at Jerusalem having been bidden to go and dwell in Pella
of Peraea by a certain oracle (κατά τινα χρησμόν) given by revelation
to those held in esteem there (τοῖς αὐτόθι δοκίμοις). Epip. (Naz. 7,
p. 123 B) speaks also of the migration to Pella, in which he includes "all the [? disciples of the] apostles[1]," and which he ascribes
to a command of Christ: in his Mens. et Pond. 15, p. 171 A, he
again refers to it, but speaks of "all the disciples," and of a divine
warning by an angel. The common source of both is not unlikely
to be Hegesippus, whom Eusebius transcribes for the account of
St James's death. That event has an uncertainty of its own. If,
as is most probable, the account in Josephus is not an interpolation,
and is true, St James's death must have occurred early in 62.
It is true that Hegesippus closely connects it with the siege
(Eus. ii. 23. 18), which was in 70: but his language need not be
interpreted chronologically. The whole account, however, of the
subsequent events is too vague to allow us to use it for determining
the particular crisis which led the apostles, or some of them, to
leave Palestine.

We are equally ignorant what course St John took, and what was
his local or ecclesiastical position when he was banished to Patmos.
The authority with which he writes is not necessarily official

---

[1] [Oehler prints τῶν μαθητῶν τῶν ἐν Πέλλῃ ᾠκηκότων, but notes in Addenda
'Pro μαθητῶν τῶν ἐν in Ven. est ἀποστόλων ἐν.']

authority: his personal position towards our Lord as one of the Twelve and one of the Three will account for everything. It is conceivable that at this time he had some definite government of the churches of Asia; but there is no evidence for it, such as we might naturally have expected had this been his position. His voice throughout is not the voice of a ruler, but of a prophet.

Although we are obliged to acquiesce in ignorance of much that we should greatly desire to know, it is quite possible to gain a clear view of the position of the Apocalypse in the Apostolic age and the Apostolic literature. Putting aside St Paul's Epistles, three great Epistles from other hands seem to belong to different stages in the eight to ten years preceding the Fall of Jerusalem, with shadows deepening as the climax approaches. These are James, 1 Peter, Hebrews; and then last of all, out of the very midst of that day of the Lord foretold by Christ Himself, we have this trumpet message to the seven churches of Asia. Thus, although the Apocalypse is not the last book of the N.T., it is the last book of that great first period which ends with God's final judgment on His own holy city. St John's Gospel and Epistles are spoken out of and into the midst of another world, the world which in a true sense is our own world or at least continuous with it. But a generation earlier, when the Apocalypse was written, St John already stood alone, the last of the great apostles: St James, St Peter, and St Paul had already perished by violent deaths: this book has thus a far more catastrophic and in that sense final character than it could have had in the closing years of the century.

Asia Minor was, there can be no reasonable doubt, the home of his later years; though this has latterly been rashly denied.

The evidence is Polycarp (ob. 155—6) according to Irenaeus (v. 20): Irenaeus writing to Florinus gives a precise account of his own early intercourse with Polycarp, and how Polycarp talked of his συναναστροφή with John and with the others who had seen the Lord, &c. (Eus. v. 20).

(*Papias* of Hierapolis is said by Irenaeus v. 33. 4 to have been a hearer of John and companion of Polycarp. This is less certain evidence because, though it may have come from independent knowledge, it *may* depend on a misunderstanding of Papias's words about the presbyter John, as Eusebius himself points out. But the supposed similar confusion in the case of Polycarp is most improbable when we read Irenaeus's very definite words.)

Polycarp again, according to Irenaeus (Eus. v. 24), had not been persuaded by Anicetus to change the paschal customs of Asia, as he had always kept them "with John the disciple of our Lord and the other apostles with whom he held converse" ($\sigma \nu \nu \delta \iota \acute{\epsilon} \tau \rho \iota \psi \epsilon \nu$).

About the same time *Polycrates* of Ephesus appeals to the tombs of apostles (Eus. iii. 31. 2; v. 24) in Asia, among them "John, who leaned on the Lord's breast, who became a priest wearing the $\pi \acute{\epsilon} \tau \alpha \lambda o \nu$, $\kappa \alpha \grave{\iota}$ $\mu \acute{\alpha} \rho \tau \upsilon s$ $\kappa \alpha \grave{\iota}$ $\delta \iota \delta \acute{\alpha} \sigma \kappa \alpha \lambda o s$, he is said to sleep at Ephesus." Apollonius (Eus. v. 18) speaks of John having raised a man from the dead at Ephesus. Later evidence abundant enough.

As evidence for an earlier death of St John is urged:

(1) Apoc. xviii. 20, as if SS. Peter and Paul were not enough.

(2) Heracleon (ap. Clem. *Str.* iv. 9, p. 595 Potter) speaks of Matthew, Philip, Thomas, Levi and many others as having made their confession by *their voice*, i.e. not by suffering, while John is not mentioned. But evidently his exile would count as suffering and $\mu \alpha \rho \tau \upsilon \rho \acute{\epsilon} \omega$ is in fact several times applied to him in this sense.

(3) Georgius Hamartolus [quoted in Lightfoot and Harmer, p. 519] seems to say that according to Papias John "was killed by Jews":—$\Pi \alpha \pi \acute{\iota} \alpha s$ $\gamma \grave{\alpha} \rho$ $\acute{o}$ $\mathrm{'I} \epsilon \rho \alpha \pi \acute{o} \lambda \epsilon \omega s$ $\acute{\epsilon} \pi \acute{\iota} \sigma \kappa o \pi o s$ $\alpha \mathring{\upsilon} \tau \acute{o} \pi \tau \eta s$ $\tau o \acute{\upsilon} \tau o \upsilon$ $\gamma \epsilon \nu \acute{o} \mu \epsilon \nu o s$ $\acute{\epsilon} \nu$ $\tau \mathring{\omega}$ $\delta \epsilon \upsilon \tau \acute{\epsilon} \rho \omega$ $\lambda \acute{o} \gamma \omega$ τ. $\kappa \upsilon \rho \iota \alpha \kappa \mathring{\omega} \nu$ $\lambda o \gamma \acute{\iota} \omega \nu$ $\phi \acute{\alpha} \sigma \kappa \epsilon \iota$ $\acute{o} \tau \iota$ $\acute{\upsilon} \pi \grave{o}$ $\mathrm{'I} o \upsilon \delta \alpha \acute{\iota} \omega \nu$ $\acute{\alpha} \nu \eta \rho \acute{\epsilon} \theta \eta$, $\pi \lambda \eta \rho \acute{\omega} \sigma \alpha s$ $\delta \eta \lambda \alpha \delta \grave{\eta}$ $\mu \epsilon \tau \grave{\alpha}$ τ. $\acute{\alpha} \delta \epsilon \lambda \phi o \mathring{\upsilon}$ $\alpha \mathring{\upsilon} \tau o \mathring{\upsilon}$ $\tau \grave{\eta} \nu$ τ. $\chi \rho \iota \sigma \tau o \mathring{\upsilon}$ $\pi \epsilon \rho \grave{\iota}$ $\alpha \mathring{\upsilon} \tau o \mathring{\upsilon}$ $\pi \rho \acute{o} \rho \rho \eta \sigma \iota \nu$ $\kappa \alpha \grave{\iota}$ τ. $\acute{\epsilon} \alpha \upsilon \tau o \mathring{\upsilon}$ $\acute{o} \mu o \lambda o \gamma \acute{\iota} \alpha \nu$, &c. In the condensed extract from Papias lately published by De Boor from an Oxford ms. it stands $\Pi \alpha \pi \acute{\iota} \alpha s$ $\acute{\epsilon} \nu$ $\tau \mathring{\omega}$ $\delta \epsilon \upsilon \tau \acute{\epsilon} \rho \omega$ $\lambda \acute{o} \gamma \omega$ $\lambda \acute{\epsilon} \gamma \epsilon \iota$ $\acute{o} \tau \iota$ $\mathrm{'I} \omega \acute{\alpha} \nu \nu \eta s$ $\acute{o}$ $\theta \epsilon o \lambda \acute{o} \gamma o s$ $\kappa \alpha \grave{\iota}$ $\mathrm{'I} \acute{\alpha} \kappa \omega \beta o s$ $\acute{o}$ $\acute{\alpha} \delta \epsilon \lambda \phi \grave{o} s$ $\alpha \mathring{\upsilon} \tau o \mathring{\upsilon}$ $\acute{\upsilon} \pi \grave{o}$ $\mathrm{'I} o \upsilon \delta \alpha \acute{\iota} \omega \nu$ $\acute{\alpha} \nu \eta \rho \acute{\epsilon} \theta \eta \sigma \alpha \nu$. In any case there must be some confusion or mistake.

Unless St John really was in Asia, it is hopeless to attempt to explain the beliefs about it; above all, those of Polycarp.

ΑΠΟΚΑΛΥΨΙΣ ΙΩΑΝΟΥ

ΑΠΟΚΑΛΥΨΙΣ ΙΩΑΝΟΥ

ΑΠΟΚΑΛΥΨΙC IHCOY XPICTOY, ἣν ἔδωκεν 1 I.

I. 1. 'Ἀποκάλυψις] Neither substantive nor verb used elsewhere in Apoc. or Ev. except in Jn. xii. 38 in quotation from Is. liii. 1. In Sir. the substantive is used for making known of secrets. In O.T. the verb often used for הלג, properly to uncover, make bare; sometimes (as in Dan.) secrets, mysteries, dreams, and also of a revelation of God Himself, 1 Sam. ii. 27; iii. 21; and (Heb. only, Gk ἐφάνη) Gen. xxxv. 7: besides Is. liii. 1 (as above), and xl. 5 (Heb.; LXX. ὀφθήσεται, where the other versions have ἀποκαλυφθήσεται). In Dan. the use is so far similar that God is spoken of as the revealer of secrets, ii. 22 &c. (LXX. as well as Thdtn.): but this is a remoter notion. In all five of the direct passages the meaning is clearly that the invisible Jehovah becomes in some sense visible to chosen persons, the covering that hides Him being withdrawn (or that hides His "arm," or His "glory").

In the N.T. the substantive seems to be used in this sense once, 2 Cor. xii. 1, ἐλεύσομαι δὲ εἰς ὀπτασίας καὶ ἀποκαλύψεις Κυρίου, where Κυρίου is probably Jehovah, though St Paul does not use Κύριος thus except with reference to something derived from the O.T. But further there are some striking resemblances to the full phrase here 'Ἀπ. 'Ι. Χ., viz. Gal. i. 12 (of the Gospel), "I neither received it from a man nor was I taught it, ἀλλὰ δι' ἀποκαλύψεως 'Ι. Χ." This is usually taken as "revelation by Jesus

Christ," but wrongly, as v. 16 shews, "when it pleased God...ἀποκαλύψαι τ. υἱὸν αὐτοῦ ἐν ἐμοὶ ἵνα εὐαγγελίζωμαι αὐτὸν ἐν τοῖς ἔθνεσιν," where the old rendering in me (cf. Col. i. 27; Ro. viii. 10; 2 Cor. xiii. 5; Gal. iv. 19) is enforced by the pleonasm which would be involved in the instrumental use of ἐν. That is, St Paul speaks of God as enabling him to have an inner vision and perception of His Son ("I am Jesus whom thou persecutest") which sent him forth as a preacher of the Gospel for all his days. With this accords the construction which is intentionally incomplete, "it came to me, it entered into me, through the revelation of Jesus Christ," i.e. the Gospel to St Paul was not a body of teaching (ἐδιδάχθην), but the whole results involved in the perception of Jesus Christ behind the veil (cf. Eph. iv. 20, 21).

It occurs again twice in St Paul (1 Cor. i. 7 τὴν ἀπ. τ. κυρ. ἡμ. 'Ι. Χ.; 2 Th. i. 7 ἐν τῇ ἀπ. τ. κυρ. 'Ι. ἀπ' οὐρανοῦ) with reference to that day of the Lord which includes both manifestation and judgement. The same conception is involved in the two passages of 1 Pet. where the phrase recurs without the article ἐν ἀποκαλύψει 'Ι. Χ. i. 7, 13, where, along with an implied reference to the great future revelation of Jesus Christ, an ἀποκάλυψις 'Ι. Χ. is apparently contemplated as brought about from time to time at an extreme season (i. 5 φρουρουμένους διὰ πίστεως εἰς σωτηρίαν ἑτοίμην ἀποκαλυφθῆναι ἐν

1—2

καιρῷ ἐσχάτῳ). And St Peter also refers iv. 13; v. 1 to the future revelation of Christ's glory, on which cf. Rom. viii. 18, 19. But a still more important if less verbal parallel is in our Lord's own words in Lk. xvii. 30 (Lot and Sodom) κατὰ τὰ αὐτὰ ἔσται ᾗ ἡμέρᾳ ὁ υἱὸς τοῦ ἀνθρώπου ἀποκαλύπτεται, where there is probably an allusion to Daniel's vision of judgement, vii. 13. Here ἀποκαλύπτεται expresses from another side the same idea as ἡ παρουσία in Mt. xxiv. 3, 27, 37, 39 (confined to this c. in the Gospels and not in the parallels), cf. 2 Th. ii. 8 τῇ ἐπιφανείᾳ τῆς παρουσίας αὐτοῦ. Under the pressure of the sufferings and terrors of that crisis men's faith in the reality of His presence might well fail. It might seem as though His resurrection and ascension were an idle tale, since He shewed himself no more to His sorely tempted servants. Then this revelation of Him is given that it may be shewn to them. Having been hidden from sight, He is seen with the veil rent away: having been supposed to be absent, He is found to be present.

To resume : as the verb is used in the O.T. for the unveiling of the hidden God to man, so both verb and substantive are used in the N.T. for the unveiling of the hidden Christ to man. There is a present unveiling of Him simply as He is, without reference to any special action of His, such as came to St Paul on his conversion. There are apparently successive unveilings of Him, successive Days of the Lord. There is, clearly indicated, a supreme unveiling, in which glory and judgement are combined.

Now, returning to Apoc. i. 1, we find that the sense thus suggested suits exactly.

It is true the more usual construction "Revelation made by Jesus Christ" is equally easy as Greek. It agrees also with the supposition that the *primary* purpose of the revelation was to disclose events, or an order of events. No one of course

doubts that an order of events, or rather perhaps of movements giving birth to events, is a principal subject of the book. But it does not follow that it is the primary subject. That the book should be called "an unveiling of Jesus Christ" agrees best not only with the more closely related language in other books of the N.T. (of course they have also the less specific sense of unveiling mysteries, to which the subjective construction has resort), but with the contents of the book itself. If events are the primary subject the epistles to the seven churches are an excrescence. If the invisible Lord is the primary subject, both parts of the book have a natural and fitting bond. Chapter i. esp. 12—18 is the first revelation of Jesus Christ and the several features of it reappear in the several seven epistles. The next part of the book (cc. iv., v.) opens with the vision of the Throne in heaven and God Most High sitting upon it, then of the Lamb that was slain and the Adoration of Him. Again in c. xix. 11—16 the rider of the white horse is seen going forth to judgement and war, His name being "The Word of God." That is, at the outset of the visions which follow the epistles we have a revelation of Jesus Christ in that form which fully expresses the double name, Jesus made both Lord and Christ, the Lamb of suffering and humility adored in heaven in the highest glory ; and again another revelation of Jesus Christ in which, though He seem to be quiescent and powerless, He goes forth in His might as King of Kings and Lord of Lords to execute judgement on the sinful nations, as in 2 Thess. i. 7 ff. Thus all the machinery of events is simply the result of His reign.

This interpretation is closely connected with the construction of the next clauses, which therefore had better be noticed now. The point is, What does δεῖξαι govern ? Usually a comma after θεός, none after αὐτοῦ :

αὐτῷ ὁ θεὸς δεῖξαι τοῖς δούλοις αὐτοῦ, ἃ δεῖ ΓενέϲΘαι

i.e. God gave the revelation to Jesus Christ absolutely, that He might shew to His servants (not it, but) ἃ δεῖ γενέσθαι ἐν τάχει. By this construction the transitive sense of ἀποκάλ. is virtually excluded as giving ἣν ἔδ. αὐτ. no intelligible sense. But the only reason for this is the obvious grammatical facility of giving the two accusatives (ἥν and ἃ) each a verb; and this difficulty vanishes if we take ἃ in apposition to ἥν, exactly as ὅσα εἶδεν *must* be in i. 2; cf. viii. 9; xvi. 3. Heinrichs is therefore right in making ἥν governed by δεῖξαι, as well as by ἔδωκεν. So also Primasius. This alone makes ἔδωκεν thoroughly satisfactory.

'Ι. Χ.] The full double name only at beginning, here and vv. 2, 4 (spurious i. 9 bis; xii. 17: also (ancient) xxii. 20), and probably (not certainly, for אA omit) the end, xxii. 21. Very common in St Paul, and indeed all Epistles (rarer in Heb.); rare and marked in first three Gospels and St John, Mt. only i. 1 [X. 'I., 18 ?], xvi. 21 probably, a crisis in the history. Mk. only i. 1. Lk. not at all. Jn. i. 17 (Prologue); xvii. 3. In Acts chiefly with ὄνομα, or in contexts which give a corresponding sense. Special force best seen in such passages as Acts ii. 36; iii. 18; iv. 26; ix. 22; xvii. 3 bis; xviii. 5, 28; xxvi. 23. But same sense implied in other books. Notice for St John Jn. xx. 31; 1 Jn. ii. 22; v. 1. It is worth observing that Jn. (the supposed Anti-Jewish Greek Gospel) is peculiarly rich in passages urging that our Lord is the Christ. The suffering and the glory (as St Peter would say) are inseparably blended throughout the Apocalypse.

ἔδωκεν] The similar idea and phrase of God *giving* His Son works to do and the like is very common in Jn. See esp. xvii. 8 (cf. for sense xiv. 10). For form v. 36 τὰ γὰρ ἔργα ἃ δέδωκέν μοι ὁ πατὴρ ἵνα τελειώσω αὐτά; xvii. 4 τὸ ἔργον τελειώσας ὁ

δέδωκάς μοι ἵνα ποιήσω. This last differs in nothing but in ἵνα and subjunctive for infinitive. This other construction recurs in Apoc., viz. iii. 9 (ποιήσω); vi. 4 after infinitive (ἐδόθη abs.); viii. 3 (ἐδόθη); ix. 5 (ἐδόθη); xiii. 12 (ποιεῖ); (xiii. 13 ποιεῖ, with accusative); xiii. 15 (ποιήσῃ [ἵνα not quite certain]); xiii. 16 f. (ποιεῖ with ἵνα bis); xix. 8 (ἐδόθη). But inf. with acc. stands by the side of ἐδόθη in vi. 4; vii. 2; xiii. 7; xiii. 15; xvi. 8: and in xiii. 14 we have a case differing from this in voice only, τὰ σημεῖα ἃ ἐδόθη αὐτῷ ποιῆσαι. Strictly therefore it is not the Revelation but the shewing of the Revelation which is given to our Lord, and thus "giving" acquires a large sense. This enlargement of sense is very perceptible in the Apoc., as iii. 8; iii. 9; viii. 3; (xiii. 16); xvii. 17; esp. xi. 3; xx. 4, corresponding in great measure to נתן. Cf. Jn. iii. 35 (v. 22). Among the above passages function or office appears for ἐδόθη in vi. 4; vii. 2; xiii. 7, 14, 15.

ὁ θεός] absol. of the Father, just as in Jn. i. 1.

δεῖξαι] As general in sense as "shew." Any kind of causing to see, literal or figurative. Used of words (λόγος LXX.) Jer. xxxviii. (LXX. xlv.) 21; Ezek. xi. 25. The exact parallels in Apoc. are iv. 1; xxii. 6 (cf. 8). Literal are xxi. 9, 10; xxii. 1 (cf. xvii. 1) as in some of the prophets.

τ. δούλοις αὐτοῦ] αὐτοῦ may be Jesus Christ's (as ii. 20 τ. ἐμοὺς δούλους): but more likely God's, as vii. 3; x. 7; xi. 18; xix. 2, 5; xxii. 3, 6. The conception of the book is not that the primary Revealer is Christ, though by the will or permission of God (ἔδωκεν); but that the primary Revealer is God, Christ being both that which is revealed and the supreme or immediate instrumental Revealer.

δούλ.] Not the prophets. They are so called x. 7 from Amos iii. 7: and

ἐν τάχει, καὶ ἐσήμανεν ἀποστείλας διὰ τοῦ ἀγγέλου

in xi. 18 they stand first followed by the holy ones and them that fear God. But the other passages prevail, and moreover one prophet alone is in question here, and the ultimate destination needs to be expressed: cf. Ezek. xl. 4.]

ἃ δεῖ γεν.] from Dan. ii. 28 f. (LXX. and Thdtn.), taken up (without ἃ) in our Lord's apocalyptic discourse in all three Gospels (Mt. xxiv. 6; Mk. xiii. 7; Lk. xxi. 9), and therefore sure to be in St John's mind. The δεῖ is doubtless what *must be* according to God's counsel: so very often in all four Gospels and in Acts.

ἐν τάχει] Common in all Greek (including LXX. and N.T.) for "shortly," "soon." In Apoc. only in ‖ xxii. 6. In a similar context Lk. xviii. 8; Rom. xvi. 20, of God's not tarrying long to deliver and avenge His people. Cf. for sense Mt. xxiv. 34 ‖ Mk. xiii. 30 ‖ Lk. xxi. 32, also here the constantly repeated ἔρχομαι ταχύ and (i. 3; xxii. 10) ὁ καιρὸς ἐγγύς. The judgement did fall then [ἐν τάχει], though it was but a part and prophecy of a whole period of judgement.

The apposition is virtually one of contents: the revealing of Jesus Christ would be at the same time and for that reason a revealing of things shortly to come to pass, the contents of the visions: and conversely the contents of the visions were all summed up in the one thought, an unveiling of Jesus Christ. It is remarkable that the corresponding phrase in iv. 1 is immediately followed by 25 verses before the first seal is opened, and any events on earth, so to speak, appear before St John's eyes. The unveiling of the eternal scene in heaven is the foundation of the passing scenes on earth.

καὶ ἐσήμ.] Practically change of construction.

ἐσήμανεν] Used three times in Jn. of symbolic indications of a manner

of death (xii. 33; xviii. 32; xxi. 19). In Acts xi. 28 (Agabus, cf. xxi. 10 f.) it is again a prophetic announcement of some sort (not xxv. 27 Festus). Not elsewhere in N.T. Though often used vaguely, it properly means strictly to shew by some sort of sign, and it is especially used of any intimation given by the gods to men, particularly with reference to the future. Heraclitus (11 Byw.) said 'Ο ἄναξ οὗ τὸ μαντεῖόν ἐστι τὸ ἐν Δελφοῖς οὔτε λέγει οὔτε κρύπτει ἀλλὰ σημαίνει (Plut. *de Pyth. Or.* 21, p. 404 &c.). Thus not literal prediction but figurative representation for warning or encouragement seems intended. So Prim.: "Dicendo *significavit* aliquid etiam futurorum et mysteriorum ostendit, nec superficie litterae nos voluit remanere contentos, quos ad mysteria altius perscrutanda *significationis* verbo fecit intentos." It has therefore special force in reference to a book of symbolic visions. This sense is analogous to that of σημεῖον in Jn.: but in Apoc. σημεῖον is probably hardly more than a wonder.

The accusative is doubtless not ἥν but ἅ: the word suits better events and movements than a single comprehensive revelation.

ἀποστείλας] The regular word for *commissioning*: exactly so xxii. 6: cf. iii. 6. Very often in this sense throughout the N.T., e.g. Jn. xx. 21 καθὼς ἀπέσταλκέν με ὁ πατήρ, κἀγὼ πέμπω ὑμᾶς. Used of angels Mt. xi. 10 (from Mal. iii. 1 ἐξαποστ.); xiii. 41; xxiv. 31 &c. The word seems inserted here to mark that this was a special and distinct message from Christ to His people in Asia. It is neither ἀποστείλας τὸν ἀγγ. nor τὸν δ. αὐτ. Ἰωάνην, but with διά and the dative. The whole process is treated as one mission, spoken of with reference to the sender.

ἀποστ. διά] So Mt. xi. 2 (true text), John πέμψας διὰ τ. μαθητῶν αὐτοῦ.

αὐτοῦ τῷ δούλῳ αὐτοῦ Ἰωάνει, ὃς ἐμαρτύρησεν τὸν 2

τ. ἀγγ.] Various angels appear in the book. This must be the angel of xxii. especially 6, 8, 16. By xxi. 9 he is seen to be one of the seven angels holding the seven bowls. The whole statement is virtually repeated in xxii. 16.

τ. δούλ. αὐτ.] The familiar O.T. title, taken up in N.T. The angel (xix. 10; xxii. 9) appears as fellow-servant of Jesus and the prophets, and here the same name is given to John as just before to all Christians of the churches of Asia. [The prophetic office and the Christian position are joined together.]

Ἰωάνει] The single ν almost confined to B D and the leaves of א written by scribe of B. But also statue of Hippolytus. Accounts for corruption Ἰωνᾶ in John i. 42; xxi. 15 ff. A few times not preserved in extant MSS. The dative -νει generally in best MSS., viz. Mt. xi. 4; Lk. vii. 18, 22; but apparently not Acts iii. 4. Here א has it.

2. ἐμαρτύρησεν] The verb (common in Ev. and Epp.) only here and xxii. (16, 18, 20). In 16 the angel is the subject, in 20 and probably 18 our Lord himself. Here it is John who bears the witness.

A difficult question, however, arises: How and when did John bear witness? That is, is he referring here to the writing of this very book or to some previous bearing of witness? If he is referring to this book, then this clause simply carries on what has been said in v. 1, adding another stage explicitly to the process, viz. John's conveyance of the revelation to the churches, just as he had received it from the angel, and the angel from Christ, and Christ from God. This interpretation is supported prima facie by the two final words, ὅσα εἶδεν, which remind us of i. 11 ὃ βλέπεις γράψον εἰς βιβλίον and i. 19 γράψον οὖν ἃ εἶδες. On the other hand St John's description of the testimony which he bore carries us in the

other direction. The construction of ἐμαρτύρησεν with the accusatives τ. λόγον τ. θεοῦ καὶ τ. μαρτυρίαν Ἰ. Χ. is a remarkable one. It cannot possibly mean that St John bore witness to the word of God and the testimony of Jesus Christ, as to things external to himself. That sense, a very common one with μαρτυρέω, always takes the dative. The accusative is never used except of the contents of the testimony borne, e.g. in Demosth. ἀκοὴν μαρτυρέω, to give hearsay testimony. The exact "cognate accusative" occurs 1 Jn. v. 9, 10 ἡ μαρτυρία ἣν μεμαρτύρηκεν, and Jn. v. 32 μαρτυρία ἣν μαρτυρεῖ περὶ ἐμοῦ. Here also μαρτυρίαν is included, but λόγον comes first.

The only other at all similar passage is one which illustrates ours in sense as well as form, 1 Ti. vi. 13. After reminding Timothy how ὡμολόγησας τὴν καλὴν ὁμολογίαν ἐνώπιον πολλῶν μαρτύρων, St Paul charges him before God who sustaineth the life of all things and Christ Jesus τοῦ μαρτυρήσαντος ἐπὶ Ποντίου Πειλάτου τ. καλὴν ὁμολογίαν, to keep the commandment unspotted &c. The whole passage is full of signs that St Paul is indirectly strengthening Timothy against probable persecution. He recalls to his mind the καλὴ ὁμολογία which he had made at his baptism in the face of many who could bear witness of it, in order to warn him that he may soon have to maintain that καλὴ ὁμολογία under a severer trial, and reminds him that he is in the presence of Him who before Pontius Pilate bore as His testimony the same καλὴ ὁμολογία, and thereby sealed His own condemnation. Had St Paul been speaking solely of what took place before Pilate, he would naturally have used μαρτυρίαν after ἐμαρτύρησεν. But his purpose was to mark the essential identity of the confession which Timothy might soon have to maintain with the Lord's own confession, and so he boldly repeats his former phrase τ. καλὴν ὁμολογίαν as a quasi-cognate accusative with ἐμαρτύρησεν, cognate in sense though not in form.

Returning now to Apoc. i. 2, we cannot but feel the similarity of thought. The most natural sense of the clause must be that the word of God, held fast by John himself and boldly spoken by John himself, and the witnessing of Jesus Christ by John himself, his confessing of Jesus Christ before men, were the actual testimony referred to in the verb ἐμαρτύρησεν.

But this comes out still more clearly when we turn to the other examples of this or closely similar phrases in the book. A similar combination of λόγος τ. θεοῦ and μαρτυρία occurs in three other places (vi. 9; xx. 4; i. 9). Twice it is definitely applied to martyrs, vi. 9 τ. ἐσφαγμένων διὰ τ. λόγον τ. θεοῦ καὶ διὰ τ. μαρτυρίαν ἣν εἶχον ("which they had," i.e. probably "which was given them to bear": cf. xii. 17; xix. 10); xx. 4 τ. πεπελεκισμένων διὰ τὴν μαρτ. Ἰησοῦ καὶ διὰ τ. λόγον τ. θεοῦ; and with these may be taken another reference to martyrdom in which λόγος and μαρτ. are coupled in another way, xii. 11 "and they overcame him διὰ τὸ αἷμα τ. ἀρνίου (i.e. sprinkled on them and enabling them to shed their own blood in like manner) καὶ διὰ τὸν λόγ. τῆς μαρτ. αὐτῶν, καὶ οὐκ ἠγάπησαν τ. ψυχὴν αὐτῶν ἄχρι θανάτου." Before we proceed to the third passage where ὁ λόγος τ. θεοῦ and μαρτ. are combined, it is well to notice two other places, where analogous language to that which we are examining is applied to faithful Christians generally, xii. 17, the dragon going forth to make war with them that keep the commandments of God and have the witness of Jesus (καὶ ἐχόντων τ. μαρτυρίαν Ἰ.); and again xiv. 12, "Here is the endurance of the Saints, them that keep the commandments of God and the faith of Jesus." "The faith of Jesus" here stands parallel to "the witness of

Jesus," and in both passages "the commandments of God" take the place of "the word of God."

The third more strictly similar passage is that which speaks of St John's being in Patmos διὰ τὸν λόγον τ. θεοῦ καὶ τὴν μαρτ. Ἰησοῦ. It is morally incredible that while διά in the two former cases is manifestly retrospective or at least not prospective (these men suffered death for the sake of the word of God and the μαρτ. i.e. because they refused to abjure the word and the testimony); it is incredible, I say, that here διά should be prospective, in order to receive (or in order to utter) the word and the testimony, together with a total change in the character of the word and the testimony. The parallelism of language leaves it practically certain that as those other men had been slaughtered because they were faithful to the word and the testimony, so it was because John had been faithful to the word and the testimony that he found himself in Patmos : in other words, he was banished for the witness which he had borne.

If this be so, it throws fresh light on i. 2. Whether there be a *direct* reference to the banishment or not, it must be a previous bearing of witness that is referred to, a bearing of witness having at least the same character as that which caused his exile. To him as a chosen disciple the responsibility for the word and the testimony in a peculiar sense belonged, for the word as he was a prophet, for the testimony as by his intimacy with our Lord he was charged with the apostolic function of witness. But word and testimony were likewise entrusted to every Christian to bear witness of in his measure : every one who suffered for the faith was suffering for the same word and testimony of which the beloved disciple was the preeminent witness.

τ. λόγον τ. θεοῦ] The Word or speech of God, what we call His revelation :

λόγον τοῦ θεοῦ καὶ τὴν μαρτυρίαν Ἰησοῦ Χριστοῦ,

cf. ἐλάλησεν of Heb. i. 1 f. It is essentially an O.T. conception, taken up and adopted throughout the N.T. It is frequently said to come to the prophets ("The word of the Lord came unto me" &c.) as the men through whom God spoke to His people: and so also the word of God came to John and he had to bear witness of it by giving prophetic utterance to it. The word of God came also of old time to the people, and so it did under the New Covenant. Cf. our Lord's pregnant words, Jn. x. 35 εἰ ἐκείνους εἶπεν θεοὺς πρὸς οὓς ὁ λόγος τοῦ θεοῦ ἐγένετο. On them, as well as on an apostle or prophet, lay the charge of maintaining it and bearing witness to it, and therefore of suffering for it. There is great significance in those words of the Parable of the Sower (Mt. xiii. 21; Mk. iv. 17), "when tribulation or persecution ariseth because of the word (διὰ τ. λόγον), straightway he stumbleth"; and in St Peter's words (1 Pet. ii. 8), perhaps founded on a reminiscence of the parable, οἱ προσκόπτουσιν τῷ λόγῳ ἀπειθοῦντες.

τὴν μαρτ. Ἰ. Χ.] We have already had occasion to refer to other passages of the book illustrative of the meaning of this phrase. One very difficult one I do not propose to discuss, but will merely say that it seems to be best explained in the same manner, xix. 10 ἡ γὰρ μαρτυρία Ἰ. ἐστὶν τὸ πν. τ. προφητείας. Only one other place, an instructive one, that of the two witnesses, μάρτυρες of God or of Christ (μου xi. 3), who prophesy 1260 days, and when they have ended their μαρτυρία are made war upon and conquered and slain by the beast from the abyss. Here the course of things ending in what we call martyrdom is clearly set forth. It is the same when we look to the other passages where the substantive μάρτυς is used. Putting aside for the present the two in which it is applied to our Lord Himself,

there remain ii. 13 Antipas ὁ μάρτυς μου, ὁ πιστός (μου), ὃς ἀπεκτάνθη παρ' ὑμῖν and xvii. 6 τοῦ αἵματος τ. μαρτύρων Ἰησοῦ.

While, however, we have here the chief origin of the name and idea of a martyr, it would be wrong to suppose that these words in the Apocalypse include the idea of suffering or death. They express simply the faithful witness borne, not the results of such faithful witness bearing. Ἡ μαρτυρία Ἰ. is not "martyrdom for Jesus," i.e. "dying for His name's sake," but the testimony borne to Him in word and work. Every man living in and by the faith of Him, and prepared to die rather than betray it, was in ancient phrase a witness of Him, a living, moving, ever visible sign and representative of Him and of what was believed concerning Him. Such a testimony could be rendered only by Christians: it sharply distinguished them from Jews. Most commonly St John couples this μαρτυρία with the simple Ἰησοῦ, the name associated with the low estate of His earthly life: here he adds to the Χρ. which makes up the Christian confession Jesus is Christ (or Jesus is Lord); always implied but here naturally expressed where the reference is to the full prophetic and apostolic testimony.

This bearing witness of the word of God and the witness of Jesus Christ had been St John's function ever since the Ascension, shared of course with the others. When the other leading apostles perished, it became still more distinctively his office. It is probably to some fresh and emphatic bearing of witness that these words refer, though in themselves they need not be limited to any particular time. The most natural explanation is that he means specially that bearing of witness which led to his banishment, though he does not designate it as

3 ὅσα εἶδεν. μακάριος ὁ ἀναγινώσκων καὶ οἱ ἀκούοντες
τοὺς λόγους τῆς προφητείας καὶ τηροῦντες τὰ ἐν
αὐτῇ γεγραμμένα, ὁ γὰρ καιρὸς ἐγγύς.

such till he has occasion to refer to it
again in *v.* 9, and then only allusively.

ὅσα εἶδεν] Since we have found the
reference of this verse to the Apocalypse itself untenable, ὅσα εἶδεν can
hardly refer to the prophetic vision
in which he saw the scenes of the
Apocalypse. It must then be a de-
fining of the special character of his
μαρτυρία Ἰ. X. His testimony was
that of an eye-witness. We see by
the Gospel and Epistles how these
thoughts of seeing and witnessing were
associated in his mind : Jn. xix. 35
καὶ ὁ ἑωρακὼς μεμαρτύρηκεν &c.: 1 Jo.
i. 1 f. ὁ ἑωράκ. τ. ὀφθ. ἡμ., ὃ ἐθεασ....
καὶ ἑωράκαμεν καὶ μαρτυροῦμεν &c.;
iv. 14 καὶ ἡμεῖς τεθεάμεθα καὶ μαρτυροῦμεν; so his disciples, apparently
repeating his favourite designation of
his own work xxi. 24 οὗτός ἐστιν ὁ μαθη-
τὴς ὁ μαρτυρῶν περὶ τούτων &c. But
that can have been no new thought
of his old age, for it was but the
repetition of cherished words of the
Lord Himself.

3. μακάριος] Common here, as in
Gospels (not Beatitudes only), from
Deut. xxxiii. 29, and especially Psalms.
No notion (1) of blessing by another,
or (2) of happiness in the sense of
feeling happy (subjective); but happiness objective, a right and prosperous
and enviable state.

ὁ ἀναγιν.] Evidently contrasted with
οἱ ἀκ., the one reader and the many
hearers. Reading aloud is therefore
meant, as often. No necessary reference to Jewish or Christian reading
of Scriptures, but rather as an intermediate agency between prophet
and people, as Baruch was to Jeremiah
(xxxvi. [xliii. LXX.] 5, 6), when he was,
like perhaps St John, shut up himself.
Cf. Col. iv. 16 ἀναγνωσθῇ παρ' ὑμῖν.

οἱ ἀκού.] as xxii. 18.

τ. λόγ. τ. προφ.] 'of *the* prophecy'

(not prophecy generally, though of
course the Greek allows either). So
probably also xix. 10. In the last
chapter, the close being reached, the
book and the demonstrative pronoun
come in, *vv.* 7, 10, 18, 19.

τηρ.] Common in the N.T. in this
figurative sense, while the LXX. chiefly
uses φυλάσσω. The meaning includes
more than obedience: it is the recognition and cherishing of them as a
permanent authority. [Cf. Ps. cxix. 11.]

γεγρ.] See *vv.* 11, 19. A frequent
word in Apoc.

ὁ γ. καιρὸς ἐγγύς] Very probably a
Jewish Messianic phrase. So Lk. xxi.
8, Ὁ κ. ἤγγικεν (just before δεῖ γενέσθαι,
cf. Mt. xxvi. 18 (μου) and Jn. vii. 6, 8.
Καιρός, the usual rendering of עֵת,
the fit, special, destined time. See
esp. Ezek. vii. 7, 12.

4. The Seven Churches. It is *possible* that the number is taken solely
from the symbolical seven which occurs
so frequently in Apocalypse and certain
that the number is marked for the
coincidence. But more likely that the
number was actually fixed by external
facts. The chain is locally congruous.
Ephesus, Smyrna, Pergamum, the
three great cities near the sea going
northward. Then turning E. and S.E.
from Pergamum comes Thyatira on
the great mercantile road to Sardis :
then going further up country, Philadelphia on the road to Laodicea, which
is almost due E. of Ephesus. It is by
no means certain that the seven were
not the seven chief towns in the
region included, which need not be
the whole political province. The only
doubt is about Thyatira and Philadelphia as regards importance. But it
is not at all unlikely (see on ii. 1) that
the cities selected were those which
shared the festival of τὸ κοινὸν Ἀσίας
for the worship of the Emperor. Of

ΙⲰΑΝΗⲤ ταῖς ἑπτὰ ἐκκλησίαις ταῖς ἐν τῇ Ἀσίᾳ· 4
χάρις ὑμῖν καὶ εἰρήνη ἀπὸ ὁ ὤν καὶ ὁ ἦν καὶ ὁ
ἐρχόμενος, καὶ ἀπὸ τῶν ἑπτὰ πνευμάτων ⌜ἃ⌝ ἐνώπιον
τοῦ θρόνου αὐτοῦ, καὶ ἀπὸ Ἰησοῦ Χριστοῦ, ὁ μάρτυς 5

4 τῶν

these (Marquardt, *Röm. Staatsver-waltung*, i. 374 f.) the known names are Ephesus, Smyrna, Pergamum, Sardis, Philadelphia, Cyzicus, and apparently Lampsacus. These last two lie too far to the N. for St John : and it is quite possible that Thyatira and Laodicea were included, though we do not happen to know the fact by coins or inscriptions.

ὁ ὤν] Taken simply as a name, as Ex. iii. 14 ; cf. Is. xli. 4.

ὁ ἦν] Merely the simplest way of putting ὁ ὤν into the past.

ὁ ἐρχ.] Probably not a mere future of symmetry, which would more naturally be ὁ ἐσόμενος, but "the coming One" ; probably including the thought of God coming to visit and to judge the earth. In the Apocalypse it is twice similarly used of God in the same triple phrase (i. 8 ; iv. 8) ; and its absence (except in some inferior authorities) in xi. 17 illustrates the meaning, for there a visitation of God is spoken of as having already come to pass, ὅτι εἴληφες τ. δύναμίν σου τ. μεγάλην καὶ ἐβασίλευσας. Possibly the term may have come from Hab. ii. 3 (LXX. ἐρχόμενος without ὁ), quoted with ὁ in Heb. x. 37. Of course the Messianic ὁ ἐρχόμενος of Mt. xi. 3 ; Lk. vii. 19 f. (and so practically the ἔρχου of Apoc. xxii. 17, 20) is not essentially different.

τ. ἑπτὰ πνευμ.] We must look to the other passages, iii. 1 ; iv. 5 ; v. 6. This last passage clearly carries us back to Zech. iv. 10. In the seven Epistles, xiv. 13, and probably xxii. 17 we have τὸ πνεῦμα. Nothing suggests seven angels or anything of that sort. Evidently the seven spirits are spoken

of as in the strictest sense Divine, and the plurality denotes the condescension and adaptation to the various ways of men. [There is danger in assuming that only one form of speech is lawful on these mysterious subjects.]

5. ὁ μάρτ. ὁ πιστός] Common Apocalyptic construction in apposition, the return to the nominative as the *casus rectus*. In sense, He is the pattern and head of all witnesses by act and word.

ὁ πιστός] Cf. ii. 10, 13 ; iii. 14 ; xix. 11. Doubtless in the O.T. sense, neither trustful nor even trustworthy, but constant, firm, such as sustains one who leans upon him. Prov. xiv. 5 has μάρτυς πιστός : but Ps. lxxxix. (lxxxviii.) 38 καὶ ὁ μάρτυς ἐν οὐρανῷ πιστός may easily have suggested the phrase : obscure both in Heb. and LXX. who put in ὁ without authority, except the Heb. order. Cf. Job xvi. 19 καὶ νῦν ἰδοὺ ἐν οὐρανοῖς ὁ μάρτυς μου. Also Is. lv. 4 ἰδοὺ μαρτύριον ἐν ἔθνεσιν ἔδωκα αὐτόν (David), ἄρχοντα καὶ προστάσσοντα ἔθνεσιν (μάρτυρα Aq. Sym.) : and very possibly (עֵד for עַד) 'the Father of witness' in Is. ix. 6. Probably there is here no reference to the idea of the Heavenly Witness for the oppressed, as in Job. The order of the three clauses suggests Christ's Human life and death, then Resurrection, then Ascension. In life and death alike He bore witness (see frequent use in Jn. and esp. xviii. 37) with perfect constancy, and became thus the First of human witnesses, whose witness was similarly required from them to the uttermost, from Stephen (Acts xxii. 20) to Antipas (Ap. ii. 13), and now it might be any of those to whom the message through John was addressed.

ὁ πιστός, ὁ πρωτότοκος τῶν νεκρῶν καὶ ὁ ἄρχων τῶν
βασιλέων τῆς γῆς. Τῷ ἀγαπῶντι ἡμᾶς καὶ λύσαντι
ἡμᾶς ἐκ τῶν ἁμαρτιῶν [ἡμῶν] ἐν τῷ αἵματι αὐτοῦ, –
6 καὶ ἐποίησεν ⌐ἡμᾶς⌐ βασιλείαν, ἱερεῖς τῷ θεῷ καὶ πατρὶ
αὐτοῦ, – αὐτῷ ἡ δόξα καὶ τὸ κράτος εἰς τοὺς αἰῶνας·
7 ἀμήν. Ἰδοὺ ἔρχεται μετὰ τῶν νεφελῶν, καὶ ὄψεται
αὐτὸν πᾶς ὀφθαλμὸς καὶ οἵτινες αὐτὸν ἐξεκέντησαν, καὶ

6 ἡμῖν

πρωτ. τῶν νεκ. (ἐκ spurious)] In
Col. i. 18 with ἐκ. The following words
shew the origin, Ps. lxxxix. (lxxxviii.)
27, 28. On τ. νεκ. cf. Acts xiii. 34;
Ro. i. 4. His Resurrection is the
pledge of the victory of down-trodden
causes, as well as of the life beyond
death.

ὁ ἄρχ. τ. βασ. τ. γ.] Again the
paradox. Trampled on by the world's
rulers, He is yet their true Lord: cf.
Ps. ii.

ἀγαπῶντι (not -ήσαντι)] Loves us now,
though He hides Himself from us.

λύσαντι] So אAC &c. against λού-
σαντι. The only approximate parallel
is vii. 14 οἱ ἐρχ. ἐκ τ. θλίψ. τ. μεγ. καὶ
ἔπλυναν τ. στολὰς αὐτῶν (cf. xxii. 14),
καὶ ἐλεύκαναν αὐτὰς ἐν τ. αἵματι τ.
ἀρνίου, partly from Gen. xlix. 11. But
the difference is great, and at all
events the reading is certain. Ἐν is
ἐν of price (Heb.), as v. 9: here we
have the effect of ransoming, there the
act as of the agent, both being united
in ἀπολύτρωσις. Cf. 1 Chr. xxi. 24
ἀγοράζων ἀγοράσω ἐν ἀργυρίῳ ἀξίῳ.
For the idea see Ps. cxxx. (cxxix.)
8. (Cf. Is. xl. 2.)

6. καὶ ἐποί....αὐτοῦ] Virtually a
parenthesis. ἡμᾶς probably right,
ἡμῖν possible.

βασιλεῖς καί] Read βασιλείαν, followed by ἱερεῖς. Apparently intended
as a literal translation of Ex. xix. 6
(otherwise 1 Pet. ii. 5, 9). A marked
transference to Christians as the Israel
of God. Cf. v. 9 and v. 10 ἐποίησας
αὐτοὺς τ. θεῷ ἡμ. βασιλείαν καὶ ἱερεῖς,

καὶ βασιλεύουσιν ἐπὶ τῆς γῆς. Also iii.
21. Collectively they are, or make
up, a kingdom, individually they are
priests.

7. 5 b, 6 are an interjected doxology.
Now St John returns to continue 5 a.
[The King comes to take His throne.]

μετὰ τ. νεφ.] A curious form, trans-
lated literally from the עִם of Dan. vii.
13: the LXX. substitutes the commoner
ἐπί, while Thdn., like St John, follows
the original strictly. Mk. xiv. 62 adds
τ. οὐρανοῦ: Mt. xxiv. 30; xxvi. 64 has
ἐπί and τ. οὐρ. Not simply that he
has a surrounding of clouds, but that
he compels all the clouds into his
retinue. The later Jews called Messiah
the Son of the Cloud.

ὄψ. &c.] From Zech. xii. 10, 12.

ἐξεκέντ.] Remarkable as being in
Jn. xix. 37, while LXX. (not other vv.)
here and here alone, have κατωρχή-
σαντο, רָקַד to pierce, confused with
רָקַד in Piel, to dance. Some MSS. and
Fathers in LXX. have ἐξεκ., but not the
best or earliest, and very possibly from
N.T. In Apocalypse probably direct
from Heb., and very possibly so in Jn.
But though St John's authorship were
probably the real cause of the coincidence, it is impossible to lean on
this as there may have been a form
of LXX. in which the usual rendering
of the Heb. was found; and if so, two
writers might both use it.

ἐπ' αὐτόν] Cannot possibly mean "because of him": doubtless as in Zech.
"over him," i.e. for him, the mourning

ΚΌΨΟΝΤΑΙ ἘΠ' ΑΥΤΟΝ ΠᾶϹΑΙ Αἱ ΦΥΛΑὶ ΤῆϹ ΓῆϹ. ναί, ἀμήν.
'Εγώ εἰμι τὸ "Αλφα καὶ τὸ "Ω, λέγει Κύριος, ὁ 8
θεός, ὁ ὢν καὶ ὁ ἦν καὶ ὁ ἐρχόμενος, ὁ παντοκράτωρ.

as for a first-born. It is not therefore wailing because of punishment on themselves that is meant, but the wailing of sorrowing repentance, the prophecy not being of vengeance but of conversion. In Zech. the reference is to the house of David and the inhabitants of Jerusalem. Here it is extended to all nations, the language used as to the families of the land (ἡ γῆ 12, κατὰ φυλὰς φυλάς 12, πᾶσαι αἱ φυλαί 14) being appropriated to the tribes of the earth, as really in Ezek. xx. 32 and even Zech. xiv. 17.

ναί, ἀμήν] Ναί almost unknown in LXX., ἀμήν only in late books (Neh., Chron.), γένοιτο being the usual rendering. Ναί represents fairly the conventional use of ἀμήν (meaning "truth"), and they might be taken as synonyms in two languages, like ἀββᾶ ὁ πατήρ. At the end of Books I.—III. of the Psalter (also IV. in LXX.) we have the reduplicated אָמֵן וְאָמֵן (in LXX. γένοιτο γένοιτο); and there would be force in a double form here, coming after the single ἀμήν of 6. But xxii. 20 clearly assigns the two words a separate force, Ναί the Divine promise, ἀμήν the human acceptance of it: and this is as clearly the sense 2 Cor. i. 20 q.v. Here then the two seem purposely brought together. Ναί seems to express affirmation or reaffirmation, Divine or human; ἀμήν human response and humble acceptance; so that ναί might be rendered "It is so" (end of Browning's Saul, "And the little brooks witnessing murmured, persistent and low, With their obstinate, all but hushed voices—'E'en so, it is so!'")

ἀμήν] "So be it." In Mt. xi. 26 the parallel ναί is apparently used as ἀμήν is here, and we are familiar with ἀμὴν λέγω ὑμῖν by the side of ναὶ λέγω ὑμῖν: but the usage of the

Apocalypse seems to be consistent. In xiv. 13 ναί is spoken by the Spirit, and in xvi. 7 by the altar.

8. This verse must stand alone. The speaker cannot be our Lord, when we consider i. 4, which makes ὁ ὢν &c. distinctive of the Father; and all Scriptural analogy is against the attribution of Κύριος ὁ θεός with or without παντοκράτωρ to Christ. The verse is thus the utterance of the great fundamental voice of the Supreme God, preceding all separate revelations concerning or through His Son.

τὸ "Αλφα καὶ τὸ "Ω] "Omega" is a comparatively modern name; the word "Αλφα (not letter) is the right reading. A natural symbol of the first and last of all things, especially with reference to the Word of God as the cause of all things (Gen. i.). The only real Jewish parallel is from Jalkut Rubeni (Schöttg. i. 1086), where a mystical sense is given to את in Gen. i. 1 &c.

ἀρχὴ καὶ τέλος] An early interpolation from xxi. 6; xxii. 13.
Read Κύριος ὁ θεός for ὁ κύριος. The common O.T. form.

ὁ παντοκράτωρ] In LXX. צְבָאוֹת (which is rendered by Σαβαώθ in 1 Sam.[4], Isaiah, and once Zech. xiii. 2 in B and some MSS.) is rendered by παντοκράτωρ in 2 Sam.[5], 1 Chr.[3] and all prophets except Isaiah, including Zechariah, very often. In Job, and Job alone, παντοκράτωρ almost always represents שַׁדַּי, a word variously rendered elsewhere but for the most part evasively. These are the only Heb. originals for παντοκράτωρ, which occurs a few times in Apocrypha but nowhere except in Jewish or Christian writers (one only metrical Cretan inscription παντοκράτωρ 'Ερμούνιε (Hermes)). In the N.T. it probably

9   Ἐγὼ Ἰωάνης, ὁ ἀδελφὸς ὑμῶν καὶ συνκοινωνὸς ἐν
      τῇ θλίψει καὶ βασιλείᾳ καὶ ὑπομονῇ ἐν Ἰησοῦ,
      ἐγενόμην ἐν τῇ νήσῳ τῇ καλουμένῃ Πάτμῳ διὰ τὸν
10   λόγον τοῦ θεοῦ καὶ τὴν μαρτυρίαν Ἰησοῦ. ἐγενόμην

is used rather etymologically than as
representing either of the two Hebrew
words, though its employment in the
LXX. gave it a kind of consecration.

In the N.T. the verb κρατέω seems
always (Acts xxvii. 13 perhaps ex-
cepted) to mean either to hold fast or
to get hold of. But παντοκράτωρ probably comes from the classical sense
to have mastery of, to control (thus
Soph. Oed. Tyr. 1522 πάντα μὴ βούλου
κρατεῖν). It would thus have special
force in this book as reminding the
faint-hearted that in spite of all ap-
pearances of a God-forsaken world, the
Ruler in the heavens was lord over
all the doings of men and controlling
them all in obedience to His Supreme
purposes. Thus it means not One who
can do anything but One who holds
together and controls all things. There
is much excellent matter on this word
and παντοδύναμος in Caspari's Quellen
zur Gesch. des Taufsymbols, iii. pp.
92 f., 205, 208—12, esp. n. 362; also
(specially for references to the Fathers)
Harnack, Patres Apost. i. 2, p. 134
(Eccl. Rom. Symbol.) and on Greeting
at beginning of Clem. Cor. (ibid. i. 1,
p. 2). Many here will know the admirable popular account in Westcott,
The Historic Faith, 215—20.

9. Ἐγὼ Ἰω.] As ἐγὼ Δανιήλ, viii. 1
&c. The insertion of the name natural
and almost necessary after v. 8.

θλίψει] Frequent in LXX., chiefly
for צַר and צָרָה: especially of persecution, as often in St Paul. Cf.
esp. 1 Th. iii. 4; 2 Th. i. 6, 7.

βασιλ.] as i. 6, v. 10, probably with
reference to the Beatitudes or like
sayings of Christ.

ὑπομ.] the link which binds θλίψ.
to βασιλ., the condition through which
θλίψ. becomes βασιλεία. See esp. Mt.

x. 22; xxiv. 13 (‖ Mk.) ὁ δὲ ὑπομ. εἰς
τέλος: Rom. xii. 12 τῇ θλίψ. ὑπομέ-
νοντες &c.

ἐν Ἰησοῦ] (not Ἰ. Χ. without ἐν)
belongs to all three, and combines
them. His θλίψις, βασιλεία, and ὑπομονή are all shared by those who are
faithful witnesses like Him and in
Him. Cf. Col. i. 14; 1 Cor. i. 4—7.
For ἐν cf. xiv. 13 οἱ ἐν κυρίῳ ἀποθνή-
σκοντες. But the phrase is more like
St Paul.

ἐγεν. ἐν] "came to be in," "found
myself in," not excluding being there
still.

τ. καλ.] probably because it was
obscure.

μαρτ.] Cf. Epict. Diss. 3. 24. 113
[ὁ Ζεὺς] ἐπὶ τούτοις με νῦν μὲν ἐνταῦθα
ἄγει, νῦν δ' ἐκεῖ πέμπει...εἰς Γύαρα πέμπει, εἰς δεσμωτήριον εἰσάγει, οὐ μισῶν·
μὴ γένοιτο, τίς δὲ μισεῖ τὸν ἄριστον τῶν
ὑπηρετῶν τῶν ἑαυτοῦ; οὐδ' ἀμελῶν, ὅς
γε οὐδὲ τῶν μικροτάτων τινὸς ἀμελεῖ,
ἀλλὰ γυμνάζων καὶ μάρτυρι πρὸς τοὺς
ἄλλους χρώμενος. Cf. 1. 29. 46 ὡς
μάρτυς ὑπὸ τοῦ θεοῦ κεκλημένος &c.
3. 26. 28 οὕτως ὁ θεὸς ἀμελεῖ...τῶν
διακόνων, τ. μαρτύρων, οἷς μόνοις χρῆται
παραδείγμασιν πρὸς τοὺς ἀπαιδεύτους;

10. If the verse stood alone, we
should be tempted to take it, "I came
to be in spirit in the Day of the Lord,"
i.e. to take ἐν πνεύματι adverbially, to
shew what manner of presence it was.
But this is excluded by the parallel
iv. 2 where there is nothing after ἐν
πνεύματι, which must therefore be the
predicate: and if so, it is likely to be
the same here (being both times preceded by ἐγενόμην), though adverbial
in xxi. 10.

ἐν πνεύματι] No exact parallel, but
sense clear; analogous to use by
St Paul, though not identical: equi-

ἐν πνεύματι ἐν τῇ κυριακῇ ἡμέρᾳ, καὶ ἤκουσα ⌐ὀπίσω
μου φωνὴν μεγάλην⌐ ὡς σάλπιγγος λεγούσης Ὁ 11
βλέπεις γράψον εἰς βιβλίον καὶ πέμψον ταῖς ἑπτὰ
ἐκκλησίαις, εἰς Ἔφεσον καὶ εἰς Cμύρναν καὶ εἰς Πέργα-
μον καὶ εἰς Θυάτειρα καὶ εἰς Cάρδεις καὶ εἰς Φιλα-

10 φωνὴν μεγάλην ὄπισθέν μου

valent to in a spiritual state (cf. Lk.
iv. 1 ἤγετο ἐν τῷ πνεύματι ἐν τῇ ἐρήμῳ;
Mk. i. 23 ἀνθρ. ἐν πνεύματι ἀκαθάρτῳ
&c.). A state in which the ordinary
faculties of the flesh are suspended,
and inward senses opened.

ἐν τ. κυριακῇ ἡμ.] The double sense
of this phrase has still to be considered,
for taking ἐν πνεύματι as a predicate
does not tie us down to the Sunday
sense : evidently it *might* be "I became in the Spirit, and so in the Day
of the Lord." For *Sunday* see a long
list of passages in Alford. But the
facts are not so clear as they seem.
First N.T. has always (unless here)
[ἡ] μία [τῶν] σαββάτων or πρώτη σαβ-
βάτου, and that not only in the Gospels,
where the old form might be expected,
but Acts xx. 7 ; 1 Cor. xvi. 2.
If the *Didaché* belongs to century I,
it contains the first clear instance of
κυριακή for Sunday, having in xiv. 1
κατὰ κυριακὴν δὲ Κυρίου συναχθέντες
κλάσατε &c. Cf. Harnack, *Didaché*,
p. 53.
There is an indirect reference to it
in Ign. *Magn.* 9 μηκέτι σαββατίζοντες
ἀλλὰ κατὰ κυριακὴν [ζωὴν] ζῶντες, where
in any case σαββ. shews some allusion
to Sunday. (Interpol., Ign. *Trall.* 9 ;
Magn. 9 ; *Philipp.* 13, have clear
usage : but date century IV.)
No other instance early in second
century. Barn. refers to the day as the
eighth day, but that is all. Justin
calls it the eighth and ἡ τοῦ ἡλίου
λεγομένη ἡμέρα (*Ap.* I. 67). Other
early writers, Clement, Polycarp, Her-
mas, are entirely silent.
Further on in century Melito (Eus.
iv. 26. 2) wrote περὶ κυριακῆς and then

there is no doubt about Dion. Cor.,
Iren., Clem. Al., Tert., Origen, so that
the name was certainly well established
before the end of the second century,
and at least existed at Antioch early
in the century. Thus there is no
certainty that the name was generally
received from the first.
As regards κυριακός, that fits Sunday
well, but the *apparent* special fitness
is delusive, arising from the techni-
cality which it is very unlikely that
the word can by then have acquired.
The other sense is less natural, but it
cannot seem impossible to anyone who
knows how freely the Fathers used
the adjective. (Of its earlier history,
before 1 Cor. xi. 20 and this place,
nothing is known.) The meaning
given by it is at least a worthy one.
We are too accustomed to connect
the idea of a Day of the Lord exclusively with judgment : disclosure,
enlightenment, revelation, as much
belongs to it (for the relation of the
two ideas cf. 1 Cor. iii. 13). The book
is a book of judgment, but its primary
purpose is to reveal Jesus Christ : the
revelation of Him is the starting-point
for all its other contents. Here then
this Day of the Lord may well include
both. To have the sight unsealed so
as to be enabled to come, as it were,
within the Day of the Lord might
well also be a result of being in Spirit.
As regards fitness here, either will
serve. The Sunday sense agrees best
with the form of sentence when compared with iv. 2 : the other sense, I
think, best with context. For Patmos
there is a reason, not so for the precise day : while the Day of the Lord

12 δελφίαν καὶ εἰς Λαοδικίαν. Καὶ ἐπέστρεψα βλέπειν
τὴν φωνὴν ἥτις ἐλάλει μετ᾽ ἐμοῦ· καὶ ἐπιστρέψας
13 εἶδον ἑπτὰ λυχνίας χρυσᾶς, καὶ ἐν μέσῳ τῶν λυχνιῶν
ὅμοιον ⌐γίὸν⌐ ἀνθρώπου, ἐνδεδυμένον ποδήρη καὶ
14 περιεζωϲμένον πρὸς τοῖς μαστοῖς ζώνην χρυϲᾶν· ἡ δὲ
κεφαλὴ αὐτοῦ καὶ αἱ τρίχες λευκαὶ ὡς ἔριον λευκόν,

13 υἱῷ

gives the key to the book. Hence I prefer this, though with some doubt.

12. λυχνίας] The Mosaic λυχνία for the Tabernacle, that which stood (one or more) in the later temples and in the vision of Zech. iv. 2 had seven branches. But as commentators point out, here we have seven distinct lampstands each with its one light. Of course nothing to do with candlesticks (due to Vg. candelabra) but a kind of lamp with a wick and oil.

13. ὅμοιον υἱόν] not here so well attested as ὁ. υἱῷ, but comparison with xiv. 14 justifies the peculiar form. Not, however, an accusative for a dative, which would be monstrous indeed, and at variance with usage of Apocalypse. But ὅμοιον virtually an adverb like οἷον. The accumulation of words denoting likeness is striking in Ezek. i., Dan. x. The actual phrase υἱ. ἀνθ. comes partly from Dan. vii. 13, partly from Ezek., but most of all now from our Lord's own words, the full force of which is seen in Jn. v. 27, which combines both the primary and the applied sense.

ἐνδεδ. ποδήρη] coincides as to Greek with Ezek. ix. 2 f., but this may be deceptive, the Heb. being בַּדִּים, an unlikely word for here. In Dan. x. 5 (a passage from which some words here seem to be taken) this בַּדִּים occurs, transliterated βαδδίν by Thdn. but rendered βύσσινα by LXX. (so also xii. 6 f.). ποδήρης is not much used in LXX. In Exod. xxviii. 4 it occurs in the list of priestly garments for מְעִיל,

the robe. In v. 31 (referring to the high-priest) ὑποδύτης ποδήρης is substituted (the Masor. addition ephod being dropped), and thenceforward ὑποδύτης is the word for מְעִיל in the Pent., several other renderings elsewhere. (ποδήρης stands elsewhere for two other unsuitable words.) But in Wisd. xviii. 24 (Aaron's) ἐπὶ γὰρ ποδήρους ἐνδύματος ἦν ὅλος ὁ κόσμος (a statement also in Philo and Jos.) and Sir. xlv. 8 again Aaron, περισκελῆ καὶ ποδήρη καὶ ἐπωμίδα (in general terms xxvii. 8 ἐνδύσῃ αὐτὸ [τὸ δίκαιον] ὡς ποδήρη δόξης). A χιτὼν ποδήρης is worn by the Jewish high-priest in Plut. ii. 672 A. Thus the biblical associations of the word are chiefly connected with the high-priesthood. What, however, makes it somewhat doubtful whether that is distinctly meant here is the absence of any other clear sign of the high-priesthood. Not improbably the conception is that of sacred repose. The work of the glorified Lord is not the kind of work for which he wore the dress of ordinary occupations. So the gods were represented in a ποδήρης, Athene, Dionysus, Niké. The colour was purple.

περιεζ....χρυσ.] Dan. x. 5 Chald. (cf. Thdn.) not LXX. (cf. xv. 6).

π. τ. μαστοῖς] Jos. Ant. 3. 7. 2 says of the high-priest's robe, ποδήρης χιτών, ὃν ἐπιζώννυνται κατὰ στῆθος, ὀλίγον τῆς μασχάλης ὑπεράνω τ. ζώνην περιάγοντες. Probably, as Trench says, for calmer, more majestic movement.

14. Dan. vii. 9; x. 6.

ὡς χιών, καὶ οἱ ὀφθαλμοὶ αὐτοῦ ὡς φλὸξ πυρός, καὶ οἱ 15
πόδες αὐτοῦ ὅμοιοι χαλκολιβάνῳ, ὡς ἐν καμίνῳ ⌐πεπυ-
ρωμένης⌐, καὶ ἡ φωνὴ αὐτοῦ ὡς φωνὴ ὑδάτων πολλῶν,
καὶ ἔχων ἐν τῇ δεξιᾷ χειρὶ αὐτοῦ ἀστέρας ἑπτά, καὶ 16
ἐκ τοῦ στόματος αὐτοῦ ῥομφαία δίστομος ὀξεῖα
ἐκπορευομένη, καὶ ἡ ὄψις αὐτοῦ ὡς ὁ ἥλιος φαίνει
ἐν τῇ δυνάμει αὐτοῦ. Καὶ ὅτε εἶδον αὐτόν, ἔπεσα 17
πρὸς τοὺς πόδας αὐτοῦ ὡς νεκρός· καὶ ἔθηκεν τὴν
δεξιὰν αὐτοῦ ἐπ᾽ ἐμὲ λέγων
   Μὴ φοβοῦ· ἐγώ εἰμι ὁ πρῶτος καὶ ὁ ἔσχατος, καὶ ὁ
ζῶν, – καὶ ἐγενόμην νεκρὸς καὶ ἰδοὺ ζῶν εἰμὶ εἰς τοὺς 18
αἰῶνας τῶν αἰώνων, – καὶ ἔχω τὰς κλεῖς τοῦ θανάτου

15 πεπυρωμένοι

15. χαλκολιβ.] practically only here and in ii. 18, for the ancient commentators evidently knew no more than we do. The only other record is a spurious sentence attributed to Suidas (εἶδος ἠλέκτρου τιμιώτερον χρυσοῦ &c.). The notion of λίβανος being the Heb. לָבַן, to whiten, is monstrous, and so are all renderings that make χαλκός the substantive participle. Nothing will serve philologically but "brasslike λίβανος." Now λίβανος is the fragrant gum of frankincense; and amber, a highly prized fragrant gum, might well be called brasslike λίβανος. The only question is whether amber itself is meant (so Ewald), or a glowing metal named from amber by this name as well as by ἤλεκτρον. Now here there seem to be two comparisons (as above the wool and the snow), the χαλκολ. and the glow of the furnace. And this recalls Ezekiel's visions, i. 27; viii. 2 (on which Origen says διὰ τοῦτο εἰσήγαγε τὸν θεὸν ἐκ πυρὸς καὶ ἠλέκτρου συνεστηκότα. In Jer. Hom. xi. p. 191). In the LXX. ἤλεκτρον doubtless means not amber, but the metal electrum, and this is probably what St John has in view. Cf. Suidas, χαλκολίβανον,

a kind of electrum more precious than gold. Now electrum is ἀλλότυπον χρυσίον μεμιγμένον ὑέλῃ καὶ λιθείᾳ.

ἐν καμίνῳ πεπυρωμένης] so AC. -νῳ not likely, being an easy correction, -νοι probably quite late, -νης very hard. Probably to agree with subaud. χαλκολιβάνου, λίβανος being sometimes feminine. Some Latin authorities, however, seem to have ἐκ καμίνου πεπυρωμένης, which is not impossible (cf. Dan. iii. passim; and ? Job xli. 11).

καὶ ἡ φω. &c.] Dan. x. 6: Ezek. i. 24; xliii. 2 Heb.

16. ἔχων] change of construction, one of a series of nominatives. So rather than ἀστέρες to bring out His holding them. ἐν here parallel to ἐπὶ 20.

ὁ ἥλιος &c.] Jud. v. 31.

17. Μὴ φοβοῦ] Dan. x. 12, 19.

Ἐγώ...ἔσχ.] Is. xliv. 6 Heb.; xlviii. 12 Heb.

ὁ ζῶν] added, forming a link and foundation.

18. a. Parenthetic, as 5b, 6.
b. τὰς κλεῖς τ. θαν. καὶ τ. ᾅδ.] (cf. Ps. vi. 6; Is. xxxviii. 10, 18). Wetstein quotes various Jewish sayings, which may be summed up "There

H. A.   2

18 THE APOCALYPSE [I. 19, 20

19 καὶ τοῦ ᾅδου. γράψον οὖν ἃ εἶδες καὶ ἃ εἰσὶν καὶ
20 ἃ μέλλει γίνεσθαι μετὰ ταῦτα. τὸ μυστήριον τῶν ἑπτὰ
ἀστέρων οὓς εἶδες ἐπὶ τῆς δεξιᾶς μου, καὶ τὰς ἑπτὰ
λυχνίας τὰς χρυσᾶς· οἱ ἑπτὰ ἀστέρες ἄγγελοι τῶν

are three keys in the hand of God, the key of the tomb (also 'resurrection'), the key of rain, and the key of childbirth."

20. μυστήριον] In N.T. only μυστ. τ. βασ. τ. οὐρ. (τ. θεοῦ) in Gospels, Paul often, and Apocalypse. In LXX. confined to Daniel, whence it probably comes here: several times in Apocrypha. Here x. 7; xvii. 5, 7. Not so much the symbolic representation as what is represented by it.

Very awkward in sense to govern τ. μ. by γράψον: better supply "is this."

ἐπί] probably, as Plumptre says, lying on the outstretched hand.

τὰς ἑ. λυχνίας] possibly by a violent attraction: more probably καί = "as thou didst also."

ἄγγελοι] Great and difficult question. Both the chief interpretations have in common the difficulty that the ἄγγελοι are apparently made responsible for the good and evil of the Churches.

Andreas refers to ὁ κύριος, i.e. probably ὁ Κύριλλος: τούτων δὲ ἑκάστῃ ἄγγελος φύλαξ ἐφέστηκε, καθώς φησιν ὁ κύριος· καὶ ὁ Θεολόγος δὲ Γρηγόριος οὕτω τὸ παρὸν νενόηκε κεφάλαιον. Possibly he means Cyr. Al. In Jo. Ev. vi. p. 638 (on x. 1—5): ὁ τεταγμένος ἄγγελος εἰς τὸ ταῖς Ἐκκλησίαις ἐπιστατεῖν, καὶ συμπράττειν τοῖς ἱερᾶσθαι λαχοῦσιν εἰς τὰς τῶν λαῶν ὠφελείας: though there is no clear reference to the Apocalypse there, only to "churches."

The most obvious sense, "angels," has in its favour the usage of the rest of the book (esp. ἀ. τῶν ὑδ. xvi. 5), the commonest use of the word in N.T. So the Greek Fathers, mostly understanding guardian angels. Orig. Hom. in Lc. xxiii. p. 961; Hom. in Num. xi. 4, p. 307; xx. 3, p. 350; 4, p. 351; De

Orat. 11. p. 214; De princ. 1. 8, 1. Greg. Naz. Or. 42 c. 9, πρὸς δὲ τοὺς ἐφεστῶτας ἀγγέλους, πείθομαι γὰρ ἄλλους ἄλλης προστατεῖν ἐκκλησίας, ὡς Ἰω. διδάσκει μὲ διὰ τ. Ἀποκ. &c. And so Andreas. Another Greek commentator in the Catenae, mixed up with Andreas, perhaps Arethas, treats the angel as the Church itself. The idea of angels answering to churches agrees with the [princes (שׂר: in LXX. sometimes ἄγγελος)] "Archons" of Daniel, in relation to nations, and is illustrated by what is said of the angels of children, Mt. xviii. 10, and even Acts xii. 15. This agrees also well enough with i. 20, the heavenly representatives in Christ's own hand, the earthly copies resting on the earth. This interpretation is also supported by the difficulty of the phrase as applied to human heads of churches; first, in respect of the form, if "messengers of churches," a phrase which would be naturally used only if the persons meant were such as corresponded to some of the subordinate officers of Jewish synagogues, a view once actually held, but now abandoned as whimsically inapplicable. If human messengers are meant, it must be assumed that the term means messengers of God. But, secondly, the difficulty is as great with reference to function as it is to name. To call men God's messengers implies their office to be representatives of God to men; whereas in the actual contents of the Epp. there is no trace of this, but only of the representatives of men before God. Some Jewish passages also tend the same way, e.g. Jalkut Simeoni ap. Wetst. "non vapulat populus, ut non cum eo vapulet deus ejus" (elsewhere princeps, = Archon), nearly so

ἑπτὰ ἐκκλησιῶν εἰσίν, καὶ αἱ λυχνίαι αἱ ⌈ἑπτὰ ἑπτὰ⌉
ἐκκλησίαι εἰσίν.

20. †...†

Midrash on Canticles xix. 3 f. Wün-
sche.

For the *ruler* sense (in ancient
times apparently confined to the later
Latins, beginning with Augustine) it
may be urged מַלְאָךְ, ἄγγελος, is used in
later books of O.T. for human prophets
as messengers of God, Hagg. i. 13; Mal.
ii. 7 &c., and Malachi himself, by a translation of his name, is commonly known
in Greek as ὁ ἄγγελος, and perhaps
the curious Eccles. v. 6, where we
have the article. The sense, though
not = ἀπόστολος, has much in common,
and heads of churches might be called
angels of Christ. The genitive ἐκκλησίας may conceivably denote his destination, the sphere of his messenger-
ship. The phrase is strange indeed on
the supposition that the substance of
each epistle really refers to the individual conduct of each ruler, as
Plumptre virtually makes it. Ewald
gives the interpretation a more tenable
form by urging that the name is given
to them simply as rulers and teachers
in the sight of God, and that in them
the individual virtues and short-
comings of the churches are summed
up as in a single head. But by far the
strongest reason for supposing human
angels is the difficulty, on the other
supposition (a difficulty which I once
felt strongly), that, *prima facie*,
St John is bidden on earth to write to
a being in heaven what is meant to
come back to the actual church on
earth.

Nevertheless, it is harder still to
believe that in Greek the ἄγγελος of a
church could mean anything but the
ἄγγελος *sent* by a church and that is
here impossible. Again, if the ἄγγελοι
are human, the definite special words
spoken to each must refer to these
men themselves, and it would be

astonishing if in all cases they were
equally applicable to the churches at
large, to which undoubtedly they were
in some sense practically addressed.
Moreover in *v.* 11 we hear of sending
"to the churches," the ἄγγελος only
coming later. It is thus easier to
believe that each church is thought of
as having its individuality, its cor-
porate unity expressed by the thought
of a representative angel in Christ's
very presence. Nor again is there any
indication of a separate writing separ-
ately sent to each church or ἄγγελος
of a church. The writing to the Seven
Churches is all included in the writing
of the one book (see *v.* 11), the whole
of which was in its turn to be com-
municated to the Seven Churches
successively. Thus the actual physical
writing would be direct to the
churches, and the interposition of
the angel as a receiver of each individual message belongs, so to speak,
to another sphere: it is ἐν πνεύματι,
as St John himself was when he be-
held the vision and heard the voice.
Hence we may safely take ἄγγελος in
its most obvious sense, angel, not
indeed as, so to speak, independent guardian angels, but as
Gebhardt expresses it (*Lehrb. d.
Apoc.* p. 40) personified spirits of the
churches, the image of their living
unity.

For "angel" Lightfoot *Phil.* 199 ff.,
Düsterdieck, Milligan, Alford, Gebhardt (39 f.) and Weiss. For "ruler"
esp. Ewald ed. 2, 124 ff., and esp.
Jahrbücher ii. 123 ff.

CHAPTERS II—III. EPISTLES TO
THE SEVEN CHURCHES.

Each epistle has a superscription
τ. ἄγγ. &c. Then it is divided into
three parts.

II. 1 $T\hat{\varphi}$ $\dot{a}\gamma\gamma\acute{\epsilon}\lambda\varphi$ $\tau\hat{\varphi}$ $\dot{\epsilon}\nu$ $\dot{E}\phi\acute{\epsilon}\sigma\varphi$ $\dot{\epsilon}\kappa\kappa\lambda\eta\sigma\acute{\iota}as$ $\gamma\rho\acute{a}\psi o\nu$
         $T\acute{a}\delta\epsilon$ $\lambda\acute{\epsilon}\gamma\epsilon\iota$ $\acute{o}$ $\kappa\rho a\tau\hat{\omega}\nu$ $\tauo\grave{v}s$ $\dot{\epsilon}\pi\tau\grave{a}$ $\dot{a}\sigma\tau\acute{\epsilon}\rho as$ $\dot{\epsilon}\nu$ $\tau\hat{\eta}$
         $\delta\epsilon\xi\iota\hat{a}$ $a\dot{v}\tauo\hat{v}$, $\acute{o}$ $\pi\epsilon\rho\iota\pi a\tau\hat{\omega}\nu$ $\dot{\epsilon}\nu$ $\mu\acute{\epsilon}\sigma\varphi$ $\tau\hat{\omega}\nu$ $\dot{\epsilon}\pi\tau\grave{a}$ $\lambda v\chi\nu\iota\hat{\omega}\nu$

1. Description of the speaker, founded, though not exclusively, on some part of i. 12 ff.

2. The body of the epistle, usually both praise and blame, praise on the whole first.

3. A distinctive promise, sometimes referring to later contents of the book. With this a warning 'Ο ἔχων · οὖς, which in the first three epistles precedes the promise, and in the last four follows it.

II. 1. τῷ ἀγγ. τῷ ἐν] (for τῆς ἐν). So AC, Prim. here (36 having τῷ τῆς). Prim. makes the curious statement, "Dativo hic casu *angelo* posuit, non genetivo (ac si diceret 'Scribe angelo huic ecclesiae'), ut non tam angelum et ecclesiam separatim videatur dixisse quam quis angelus exponere voluisset, unam videlicet faciens angeli ecclesiaeque personam." The remark is doubly interesting as inconsistent with his own interpretation of ἄγγελοι as *rectores populi*. Probably he borrowed here from an earlier commentator. In ii. 8, 18 there is also sufficient authority. In iii. 1, 7 some but not sufficient. In ii. 12 mere indications. But probably all had once the same. Now it is very curious that the high priest of the Augustan worship in the great cities of Asia appears always in Inscriptions with an analogous formula. Thus

$$\dot{a}\rho\chi\iota\epsilon\rho\epsilon\grave{v}s\ '\text{A}\sigma\acute{\iota}as \begin{cases} \nu a\hat{\omega}\nu\ \tau\hat{\omega}\nu \\ \nu ao\hat{v}\ \tauo\hat{v} \end{cases} \dot{\epsilon}\nu\ '\text{E}\phi\acute{\epsilon}\sigma\varphi.$$

In no case that I have seen is there τοῦ or τῶν before ναοῦ (-ῶν). It is not at all unlikely that St John intended to contrast the poor persecuted little Christian congregations, spiritual churches, with the stately temples and worship in honour of monsters like Nero. [See detached note pp. 38 ff., also Westcott and Hort App. pp. 136 f.]

The construction is probably "the

angel that is in Ephesus, the angel of a church," i.e. ἐκκλησίας being used in a quasi-adjectival sense. This at least is easier than ἐν Ἐ. ἐκκ. for τῆς ἐν Ἐ. ἐκκ.

Ἐφέσ.] Ephesus needs less to be said of it than any of the others, as it is so familiar in N.T. and so much written about. St Paul's great resting-place after Antioch, and the one great Christian capital of his own founding. Thence he wrote 1 Cor., to it Eph. and also 1 Tim. Further it is connected with all St John's writings. Plumptre does well to use 1 Tim. in illustration: but even if the ἄγγ. ἐν Ἐφ. were a human ruler Timothy could hardly be meant. Lightfoot is certainly right in supposing Timothy's office to have been temporary, and St Paul's urgent entreaty (σπούδασον *bis*) to him to come to him "quickly," "before winter" (2 Tim. iv. 9, 21), is marked, though of course the request may have remained unfulfilled.

Τάδε λέγει] perhaps from Am. i. 6 &c.

ὁ κρατ. &c.] The central church of Asia is addressed by the Lord in His so to speak central function in relation to the churches, as holding all seven together, making them one in Him. It was also what St John first saw. The stars which (i. 16) he "had" in His right hand appear here as "held" in it; so that they cannot be taken away. So conversely in v. 13 the angel of Pergamum holds fast Christ's name.

περιπατῶν] is a new point, cf. iii. 4. Considering the allusion to the garden in v. 7 it is quite possible this may have some reference to Gen. iii. 8, 10; but not certain. The conception is doubtless that of Lev. xxvi. 12 (cf. Deut. xxiii. 14), quoted by St Paul 2 Cor. vi. 16, "I will dwell in them and walk in them"; cf. 2 Sam. vii. 6 f.; 1 Chron. xvii. 5 f. Doubtless life and

τῶν χρυσῶν, Οἶδα τὰ ἔργα σου, καὶ τὸν κόπον καὶ 2
τὴν ὑπομονήν σου, καὶ ὅτι οὐ δύνῃ βαστάσαι κακούς,
καὶ ἐπείρασας τοὺς λέγοντας ἑαυτοὺς ἀποστόλους,
καὶ οὐκ εἰσίν, καὶ εὗρες αὐτοὺς ψευδεῖς· καὶ ὑπο- 3
μονὴν ἔχεις, καὶ ἐβάστασας διὰ τὸ ὄνομά μου, καὶ

motion in and among the seven churches is represented by the seven lampstands: a sharing of their life and motion is intended.

2. Οἶδα τὰ ἔργα σου] spurious for Smyrna and Pergamum. Found in the other five (σου τὰ ἔ.). The two exceptions refer to special trials of circumstance. ἔργα seems used in great generality if we take all the epistles together, both good and bad. Principally actions.

κόπον] never mere work, but laborious work, toil, as 1 Cor. xv. 58. (μόχθος, in N.T. employed only *in addition* to κόπος (Paul[3]), seems used as a stronger word than κόπος.) Apparently extended to painful, anxious life, as sometimes עָמָל, which is often rendered κόπος in LXX. Cf. xiv. 13, rest from their labours.

ὑπομονή] as towards outward trial and persecution; an inward feeling as well as outward conduct, but directed only towards aggression. Hence it is the way in which the κόπος is met.

βαστ.] to carry a burden, not (as such) to tolerate. The only known passage at all approaching it is Epict. i. 3, 2, ἀλλ' ἂν μὲν Καῖσαρ εἰσποιήσηταί ("adopt") σε, οὐδείς σου τ. ὀφρὺν βαστάσει ("be able to stand"). The force here is shewn by *v.* 3, "thou canst bear the burden of persecution, but not that of evil men as brethren: ὑπομονή, yes; but not such as would endure κακοί" &c.

κακούς] not wicked, but evil, as opposed to good. A less *personal* word than πονηρός, referring to quality rather than guilt, implying that a man is not what for some reason or

other he was meant to be; hence (Mt. xxiv. 48) κακὸς δοῦλος and (Phil. iii. 2) τ. κακοὺς ἐργάτας, applied to the same sort of men (Mt. xxi. 41 κακοὺς κακῶς ἀπολέσει αὐτούς is the only other personal κακός or -οί in N.T. and there γεωργούς is virtually understood). But here probably in the looser LXX. sense of "evil" generally. Curiously the only other place in Apocalypse for either κακός or πονηρός in xvi. 2 (ἕλκος).

τ. λέγ. ἑαυ. ἀποστ.] This is one of the passages supposed to shew antipathy to St Paul. No doubt that (e.g. in Gal.) he has occasion to plead his apostleship against Judaizers, 1 Cor. ix. 2; 2 Cor. xi. 5 = xii. 11; xii. 12; and two or three passages in *Hom.* *Clem.* at a much later time shew a very bitter feeling against him and his claims. But St Paul himself had occasion to say in like manner of others that they were pseudapostles, no apostles of Christ (2 Cor. xi. 13 f.), doubtless Judaizers. The words here may just as well apply to Judaizers, or indeed to any who put forward false claims to apostleship. (Cf. 9; iii. 9.)

3. He resumes from 2a: the ὑπομονή there spoken of needed fresh and emphatic recognition.

διὰ τ. ὄν. μου] Coming therefore under such words of the Lord as Mt. x. 22; xxiv. 9; with each of which passages ὁ ὑπομείνας &c. is associated.

κεκοπίακες] The proper classical sense is to be weary, and so in Jn. iv. 6, and very possibly Mt. xi. 28. The usual N.T. sense is to labour to weariness (κόπος). Here to be weary morally, i.e. to allow oneself to become weary. Cf. for *sense* Gal. vi. 9 ἐκλυόμ., Heb.

4 οὐ κεκοπίακες. ἀλλὰ ἔχω κατὰ σοῦ ὅτι τὴν ἀγάπην
5 σου τὴν πρώτην ἀφῆκες. μνημόνευε οὖν πόθεν
πέπτωκες, καὶ μετανόησον καὶ τὰ πρῶτα ἔργα
ποίησον· εἰ δὲ μή, ἔρχομαί σοι, καὶ κινήσω τὴν
λυχνίαν σου ἐκ τοῦ τόπου αὐτῆς, ἐὰν μὴ μετανοήσῃς.
6 ἀλλὰ τοῦτο ἔχεις ὅτι μισεῖς τὰ ἔργα τῶν Νικολαϊτῶν,

xii. 3, 5. 2 Sam. xvii. 2 associates (in literal sense) κοπιῶν καὶ ἐκλελυμένος χερσί. For the word in this sense cf. Jer. xvii. 16. But also classical. Epicurus ap. Clem. *Str.* iv. p. 594 μήτε νέος τις ὢν μελλέτω φιλοσοφεῖν μήτε γέρων ὑπάρχων κοπιάτω φιλοσοφῶν. Themistocl. (to the Athenians) ap. Plut. ii. 185 F, τί κοπιᾶτε ὑπὸ τῶν αὐτῶν πολλάκις εὐχρηστούμενοι;
Omit καὶ οὐ κέκμηκας, apparently an invention of Erasmus, through misunderstanding of κεκοπ.

4. τ. ἀγάπ. σ. τ. πρ.] Not = τ. πρώτ. ἀγ. σου, but should be "Thy love, thy first love," "thy love, that first or original love of thine." There is no indication that the love meant has any reference to any espousal of the Church to Christ (cf. Jer. ii. 2 ; 2 Cor. xi. 2). It is more probably the characteristic ἀγάπη of Christian brotherhood, which poured itself forth in the first fervour of their faith. Cf. 1 Th. i. 3; iii. 6; 2 Th. i. 3; Phil. i. 9; Col. i. 4 [Mt. xxiv. 12]. Despite good acts and other good feelings, love was wanting, though it had been present. That such declension of mutual love presupposed declension of love towards God, would be recognised at once by every Christian. Then τ. πρώτην marks it as the characteristic of the earliest Christian state of Ephesus. Contrast *v.* 19. There is no force in Trench's contrast of this censure with the absence of censure in Ephesians, and consequent inference that a generation must have intervened. The years that had intervened before the earlier date of the Apocalypse were few, but eventful and disturbing.

5. τὰ πρῶτα ἔργα are the characteristic works of love. Cf. τοῦ κόπου τῆς ἀγάπης 1 Th. i. 3.
ἔρχομαί σοι] not πρός σε (? not שׁ). So Zech. ix. 9 ap. Mt. xxi. 5. Virtually a dat. commodi or incommodi. "I come to thy concern," "thou wilt find me coming."

6. There is nothing to shew that this has anything to do with *v.* 2, λέγ. ἑαυτ. ἀποστ. On the other hand, ii. 14 f. shews what the Nicolaitan teaching was, viz. of a lax and libertine kind.
In Acts vi. 5 we have simply Νικόλαον προσήλυτον Ἀντιοχέα.
The Fathers have contradictory accounts about Nicolaus, and his connexion with a supposed sect of Nicolaitans. The earliest is in Clem. Al. *Str.* iii. 522 f. (cf. ii. 490 f.). He tells how it was said, φασί, that Nicolaus being rebuked by the apostles for jealousy about his beautiful wife brought her into the midst for any one that pleased to marry, that he married no one else, and that his daughters lived unmarried &c. Clement calls him an "apostolic man." He quotes as his the phrase δεῖν παραχρῆσθαι τῇ σαρκί, saying that Nicolaus meant by this κολούειν the pleasures and desires, but that the men of his sect gave the words a wrong sense as a sanction for their own immorality. He adds that Matthias likewise taught σαρκὶ μὲν μάχεσθαι καὶ παραχρῆσθαι &c. In Herodotus παραχρῆσθαι means to despise, treat lightly: but there are no other known examples of this sense. The common sense is to *misuse* (as Aristotle and Philo) and specially of immoral misuse of the

ἃ κἀγὼ μισῶ.   Ὁ ἔχων οὖς ἀκουσάτω τί τὸ πνεῦμα 7

body, so that the sect's interpretation
was by no means forced. But Just.
Ap. i. 49 says that the Jews παρε-
χρήσαντο our Lord (which does not,
as some say, = διεχρήσαντο, but) *ill
used* Him ; and this shews that the
innocent sense indicated by Clement
is quite possible. But the probability
is that the story comes from some
apocryphal narrative, and Matthias'
name is suspicious. Clem. is copied by
Eus. iii. 29, who speaks of no other
account. So also Thdt. *Haer. fab.*
iii. 1, who avowedly follows Clement
here, as giving a σαφέστερον account.
This favourable view of Nicolaus himself is also implied in *Ap. Const.* vi. 8;
Ps.-Ign. *Trall.* 11 ; *Philad.* 6; also
" Victorin." &c. Acc. to Ewald *Gesch.*
vii. 172 Hippolytus in Lagarde *Anal.
Syr.* 87 f. speaks of Nicolaus as a
forerunner of Hymenaeus and Philetus.

Iren. I. xxvi. 3, on the other hand,
says briefly the Nicolaitae have for their
master Nicolaus, one of the seven &c.,
who " indiscrete vivunt," and then he
refers to Apocalypse. Probably there
is here no knowledge of any sect except
from Apocalypse ; and no tradition
about the man, but conjectural con-
junction of the two. A very similar
statement occurs in Hipp. *Haer.* vii.
36. Tert. refers to an evidently contemporary immoral sect of Nicolaitans,
*Praesc.*33; *Marc.*i. 29; and apparently
Pud. 19, but leaves Nicolaus himself
unnoticed.

The lost *Syntagma*, however, of
Hippolytus must have had something
more, as appears by comparison of
Epiph. xxv., Philast. 33, and Ps.-Tert.
adv. omn. haer. 1. Evidently there
was a contemporary Gnostic sect (for
Gnostic cosmographical doctrines are
mentioned by Ps.-Tert.) for which
through the Apocalypse Hippolytus
made Nicolaus responsible. But further Epiphanius had access to some
other tradition, having affinity to that
quoted by Clement but giving it

another turn, and apparently beginning earlier in the story. Both, as
Lips. *Epiph.* 104 remarks, have the
ζηλοτυπία. But (without going into
particulars) Epiph. may really have
had the same story, and misinter-
preted it after his fashion.

The whole ends in smoke. Evidently
there was a legendary book, which
gave the story of Nicolaus. Evidently
also a libertine Gnostic sect at the beginning of the third century misused
a phrase of it. But the connexion of
either with each other historically, or
of either with the Nicolaitans of
Apocalypse, is most problematical.

We are therefore reduced to the text
of Apocalypse. Now ii. 14 f. have given
rise to a popular notion that Νικόλαος
is only a Greek rendering of Βαλαάμ.
In itself the etymology is not purely a
modern invention. Buxt. *Lex.* 314
says " Rabbini ludunt de eius nomine
quod sic dictus fuerit quasi עַם בְּלַ‍ע."
But it is needless to examine what
Balaam means; Νικόλαος could never
be the *Devourer* or *Destroyer* of the
people: and moreover the way the two
names are used excludes their identity : nor would St John have gratui-
tously bewildered his readers with a
riddle which they could not possibly
understand.

There must then have been some
followers of some Nicolaus, but there
is no reason to suppose that he was
identical with the Nicolaus who was
one of the Seven. The name is ex-
tremely common.

7. ὁ ἔχων οὖς] cf. Mt. xi. 15 &c.

τὸ πνεῦμα] complementary to Τάδε
λέγει used of Christ. These epistles are
not merely a repetition of words spoken
by Christ to John in vision, but in
speaking them he is moved by the
prophetic spirit.

ταῖς ἐκκλησίαις] The special message to each separate church is also
intended for the instruction of all.

λέγει ταῖς ἐκκλησίαις. Τῷ νικῶντι δώσω αὐτῷ φαγεῖν ἐκ τοῦ ξύλου τῆς ζωῆς, ὅ ἐστιν ἐν τῷ παραδείσῳ τοῦ θεοῦ.

7 μου

Whether St John contemplated ultimate communication to churches of other lands, we cannot tell.

τ. νικῶντι] Usage very singular. In LXX. only three times, all different words, and all incorrect renderings; νίκη once only. No corresponding transitive Hebrew verb. What comes nearest is יָכֹל to prevail (against), almost always rendered, too literally, by δύναμαι in LXX. In N.T. only Lk. xi. 22 (trans.); Romans (iii. 4 from Psalms), xii. 21 bis, and *St John's writings*, the primary place being the one in the Gospel xvi. 33, ἐγὼ νενίκηκα τὸν κόσμον: six times in Epistles, altogether nine in Apocalypse, besides the seven for the Seven Churches, some transitive, others absolute. The use in v. 5 (ἐνίκησεν ὁ λέων...ἀνοῖξαι) confirms the impression that St John took νικάω as a more forcible and direct equivalent of יָכֹל: in xv. 2 (τ. νικῶντας ἐκ τ. θηρίου &c.) the construction is very odd. In Apoc. xi. 7; xiii. 7 (quotations) it represents the same root יְכֹל in Dan. vii. 21, τροπούμενον LXX., ἴσχυσεν πρός Thdn. If we take the Hebrew conception, it is that of a trial of strength, and final preponderance. The contrast of apparent and real victory implied in xi. 7; xiii. 7 X xii. 11; xvii. 14. It is possible, judging by v. 10 and iii. 11, that there may be also some association with the νικάω of Greek games, which meets us on countless inscriptions.

φαγ. ἐκ τ. ξύλου &c.] Temple, *Rugby Serm.* 25, says:—"The blessings of Paradise before the Fall, of deliverance from the Flood, of the manna in the wilderness, of the triumphs of Solomon's vast empire, are promised to the first four churches; the blessings of Baptism, of Church membership, of a seat in the great Court of Justice which is to judge the world, are promised to the last three. Thus covering the whole space from the Creation to the Judgment day, and making the Seven Churches correspond with the entire range of God's government of mankind. In this scheme then the Church of Ephesus occupies the place of the Garden of Eden, and has the blessings and the dangers, the weakness and the strength, of the dwellers in that garden. It is the type of the first love, not of the last love" &c. Essentially a true statement though needing correction. Here it is well to remember that the tree of life was not to be eaten prematurely. Now it is announced distinctly as the reward of victorious conflict, to be won, not to be snatched. Cf. ii. 10 ‖ Jam. i. 12.

παραδείσ.] The Aryan word used Gen. ii. 8 &c., in the LXX. for גָּן, also transliterated into Hebrew Cant. iv. 13; Neh. ii. 8; Eccl. ii. 5. The proper meaning of each is a place fenced or walled in. See Dillm. on Gen. ii. 8, who gives the Old Bactrian *pairi-daêza*, in Arm. *pardes*. Three times in N.T., Luke xxiii. 43; 2 Cor. xii. 4, and here. For our purpose it is simply the Garden of Eden, which reappears thus symbolically at the end of the divine course of things. The thing, though not the name, recurs xxii. 2 f., the garden as well as the city; and on each side of the river is a Tree of Life (cf. Ezek. xlvii. 12). The elaborated and thickly aggregated home of man after a process of civilisation set down in the midst of the enclosure of the fresh world of nature from which his ideal history takes its first start.

παραδ. τ. θεοῦ] taken from Ezek. xxviii.

Καὶ τῷ ἀγγέλῳ τῷ ἐν Cμύρνῃ ἐκκλησίας γράψον 8
Τάδε λέγει ὁ πρῶτος καὶ ὁ ἔσχατος, ὃς ἐγένετο
νεκρὸς καὶ ἔζησεν, Οἶδά σου τὴν θλίψιν καὶ τὴν 9
πτωχείαν, ἀλλὰ πλούσιος εἶ, καὶ τὴν βλασφημίαν ἐκ
τῶν λεγόντων Ἰουδαίους εἶναι ἑαυτούς, καὶ οὐκ εἰσίν,
ἀλλὰ συναγωγὴ τοῦ Cατανᾶ. ⌜μὴ⌝ φοβοῦ ἃ μέλλεις 10
πάσχειν. ἰδοὺ μέλλει βάλλειν ὁ διάβολος ἐξ ὑμῶν
εἰς φυλακὴν ἵνα πειραcθῆτε, καὶ ⌜ἔχητε⌝ θλίψιν
ἡμερῶν δέκα. γίνου πιστὸς ἄχρι θανάτου, καὶ δώσω
σοι τὸν στέφανον τῆς ζωῆς. Ὁ ἔχων οὖς ἀκουσάτω 11

10 μηδὲν | ἔξετε ν. ἔχετε

13; xxxi. 8, brings out the central character of it; see xxii. 1 (θρόνου &c.), 3, 5. His presence is its consecration. The term Eden, delight, does *not* appear in Apocalypse, so that what is conveyed by the term "paradisaical" is misleading: God, not delight, supplies the characteristic. (μου probably spurious here though early; comes from iii. 2, 12.)

It seems at least possible that here, as elsewhere, there is an allusion of contrast to familiar heathen objects. The παράδεισος τοῦ θεοῦ may conceivably stand over against the vast sacred τέμενος of the temple of Artemis at Ephesus. Whether the Tree of Life had any analogue, we cannot tell.

8. *Smyrna.* Blakesley (in S.D.B.) probably fanciful in connecting v. 8 with the revival of Dionysus. There may be some fitness to the place in the title chosen: but we do not know it.

9. βλασφ. ἐκ] (so read) blasphemy proceeding from, i.e. set on foot by them. Probably a reference to the inveterate enmity of the Jews, egging on the heathen against Christians.

λεγ. Ἰουδ. εἶν. ἑαυτ.] (=iii. 9). Again urged as against St Paul, and again paralleled by his own language, Rom. ii. 28 f. The Jews who refuse the hope of Israel and reject their true King have lost their title to the name of Jews. After the destruction of Jerusalem and God's manifest judgement on the nation this form of language lost its meaning. Henceforth Jew and Christian stood opposed to each other, and hence the language of St John's Gospel.

συναγ. τ. Σατ.] (=iii. 9) not synagogue of Jehovah, Num. xxvii. 17 &c. Even in N.T. συναγ. is often not the building but the congregation. On the idea cf. Jn. viii. 44 f. There the two features are lying and murder, which are the two characteristics of false accusers bringing death on Christians.

10. ὁ διάβ.] change to Greek probably for sake of sense. The same double force, with same indirect reference to human calumny, in Jn. vi. 70; viii. 44; (1 Tim. iii. 6, 7; 1 Pet. v. 8 and perhaps elsewhere).

πειρασθ....ἡμ. δέκα] Dan. i. 12, 14. A time not of the shortest and yet short, cf. Num. xi. 19, but especially the term fixed and limited by God, cf. Mt. xxiv. 22. ἵνα expresses *God's* purpose.

ἐξ ὑμῶν] some of you. So iii. 9; xi. 9.

τ. στέφ. τ. ζωῆς] Very singular that we have this in Jam. i. 12. Probably a Jewish phrase founded on O.T. analogies, though not actually in O.T. At all events the coincidence shews no using of either Apocalypse by Jam. or

τί τὸ πνεῦμα λέγει ταῖς ἐκκλησίαις. Ὁ νικῶν οὐ μὴ
ἀδικηθῇ ἐκ τοῦ θανάτου τοῦ δευτέρου.

vice versa. ζωῆς is of course suggested by θανάτου. The true end of faithful death is its seeming opposite life, bestowed by the invisible Judge looking on at the struggle. The crown is therefore apparently as usual the victor's crown, cf. 2 Ti. iv. 7, 8. But this was only one of various crowns or chaplets that would be familiar at Smyrna. Every one would think at once of the crowns worn by the sacrificing priests, in whose persecution the Christians would be as victims. Also the chief cities of Asia had their στεφανηφόροι priests, wearing golden στέφανοι. Blakesley is, I believe, wrong in saying it was a Smyrnaean custom to *present* a crown at the end of the year of office. He gives no reference but probably means Philost. *V. S.* 26 (267. 29 f.) of the sophist Heracleides, that he held among the Smyrnaeans τὴν στεφανηφόρον ἀρχήν from which (so it seems) the Smyrnaeans give the names to the years. But such offices were not peculiar to Smyrna. The word is also illustrated by Philost. *V. S.* 25 (227. 13) that the Smyrnaeans piled πάντας τοὺς οἴκοι στεφάνους on the head of Polemon: and 21 (219. 8) that Scopelianus was ἀρχ. τῆς Ἀσίας himself and all his ancestors, child from father, ὁ δὲ στέφανος οὗτος πολὺς καὶ ὑπὲρ πολλῶν χρημάτων. Also Epict. i. 19. 26 f.: "Today a certain person was talking to me on behalf of the priesthood of Augustus. I say to him, Man, let the matter alone, you will spend much to no purpose...'But I shall wear χρυσοῦν στέφανον.' If you ever desire a στέφανος, get one of roses and put it on, for it will be prettier to look at."

11. ἀδικηθῇ] no necessary sense of injustice, simply "hurt." So Lk. x. 19; Ap. vi. 6; vii. 2 &c. The LXX. evidence is unsatisfactory, being isolated and referring to injuries which were also

de facto unjust. But it is a common idiom in good Greek in certain cases. Thus Thuc. and Xen. use the word of laying waste a land. Also a wild beast biting a man is said ἀδικεῖν him in many authors. Also said of things eaten that disagree, and of frost injuring vines.

A curious case is 2 Pet. ii. 13, where the best MSS. have ἀδικούμενοι μισθὸν ἀδικίας.

Perhaps the nearest parallel is of lightning. Plut. *Quaest. Conv.* 4. 2 (p. 665 B), lightning ἀνθρώπου τε καθεύδοντος διαπτάμενος οὔτ' αὐτὸν ἠδίκησεν οὔτε τῆς ἐσθῆτος ἔθιγεν, but fused some coins attached to his belt; and *ib.* (p. 666 B) on the theory that sleepers are not struck, on account of the body being in a laxer state, and so not offering resistance to the lightning, ἧττον ἀδικεῖται τὰ εἴκοντα τῶν ἀνθισταμένων.

So too here the idea literally expressed seems not to be that such an one will not be touched by the second death, but that he will pass through it unharmed ; cf. Is. xliii. 2.

τ. θαν. τ. δευτ.] A common Jewish phrase denoting a second and retributive death in the future state. Apparently a very indefinite conception. In Baba bathra on Prov. xi. 4 (Wetst. Schöttg. 1137) it is distinguished from the judgement of Gehenna. Philo also, *de praem. et poen.* 12, p. 419, says θανάτου διττὸν εἶδος, one κατὰ τὸ τεθνάναι, good or indifferent, τὸ δὲ κατὰ τὸ ἀποθνήσκειν, ὁ δὴ κακὸν πάντως, καὶ ὅσῳ χρονιώτερον βαρύτερον, with more to the same effect. Plut. probably representing a Neopythagorean doctrine has also the phrase ὁ δεύτ. θάν. (*de fac. in orbe lunae* 27 fin.; cf. 28). When asked to explain the phrase, the expositor says that man is not, as commonly supposed, composed of two things only, body and soul, but three,

Καὶ τῷ ἀγγέλῳ ⌜τῆς⌝ ἐν Περγάμῳ ἐκκλησίας 12
γράψον
Τάδε λέγει ὁ ἔχων τὴν ῥομφαίαν τὴν δίστομον
τὴν ὀξεῖαν Οἶδα ποῦ κατοικεῖς, ὅπου ὁ θρόνος τοῦ 13

12 †...†

body, soul and νοῦς (elsewhere, De gen.
Soc. 22, p. 591, he speaks of νοῦς as
the popular name, δαίμων as the truer,
ὡς ἐκτὸς ὄντα), and that as the first
death is the separation of body and
soul, including νοῦς, so the second is
the separation of soul and νοῦς, and
this takes place gently and slowly.

But neither Jewish nor Pythago-
rean usage is a safe guide to the meaning of doctrinal terms in the Bible.
Apart from the contents of the phrase
itself, we have two indications, the
latter part of Apoc., and the place in
the series of promises. It occurs xx. 6,
14; xxi. 8, and there twice we are
told that it is ἡ λίμνη τοῦ πυρός, not
immersion in it, but the lake itself.
In xxi. 8 the neuter ὅ might leave
some ambiguity, but there is none in
xx. 14. Further, this lake of fire is
said to burn with fire and brimstone
(xix. 20; xx. 10; xxi. 8). Now the
source of this imagery is Gen. xix. 24,
of which Ezek. xxxviii. 22 (Gog and
Magog) is an echo: cf. Is. xxx. 33.
We are thus sent back to the destruction of Sodom.

Then as to the order of promises,
the second death stands between the
Garden of Eden and the Manna. It
might thus be either the Deluge, as
Bishop Temple implies, well called the
Second Death in contrast to the ex-
pulsion from the Garden. It probably
is a combination of the Deluge and
Sodom, the Waterflood and the Fire-
flood. Cf. 2 Pet. ii. 5, 6; Jude 7 (πρό-
κεινται δεῖγμα πυρὸς αἰωνίου δίκην ὑπέ-
χουσαι), i.e. a new or second deluge or
death of the world, but this time, of
fire. The Jews often associated the
two together, and the antithesis is

really involved in that of the baptism
with fire. Mt. iii. 11 ‖ Lk. iii. 16: cf.
Mk. ix. 49.

There is nothing known about
Smyrna itself that would specially
suggest this sense: but the promise
itself is negative only, viz. of a deliverance, so that the suggestion may come
from the threatened "death" of v. 10.

12. Περγάμῳ] -ον is the right form
(-ος rare [see H.D.B, not in inscr.]),
"longeque clarissimum Asiae Pergamum," Plin. H. N. 5. 30.

τ. ῥομφ. τ. δίστ. τ. ὀξ.] cf. xix. 15;
Heb. iv. 12. This probably has some
local reference, which may hereafter
be ascertained. Outside the city was
a famous temple and τέμενος of Ζεὺς
Νικηφόρος, mentioned in many writers.
If he was represented holding a sword,
this would explain everything, and
agree with the picture in xix. But
I can find no evidence as to the statue.
On some coins of Pergamum a sword
is mentioned with the serpent.

13. Οἶδα ποῦ κατοι.] Again no ἔργα,
but the difficult position.

ὁ θρόν. τ. Σατ.] θρόν. a chair of state,
implying some special authority or
consecration. Doubtless those are right
who refer this to the serpent-worship
attached to Asclepius. On every side
in Pergamum the serpent would be
seen (κατοικεῖ, 13), and it was associated with the commanding worship.
Not that he means precisely that at
Pergamum was the throne of the serpent: but the visible supremacy of
the serpent was to him a symbol of
the invisible supremacy of the power
of evil, inspiring to evil. In xii. 9
St John identifies ὁ Σατ. with ὁ ὄφις ὁ
ἀρχαῖος. There was much Ophitic wor-

Σατανᾶ, καὶ κρατεῖς τὸ ὄνομά μου, καὶ οὐκ ἠρνήσω
τὴν πίστιν μου καὶ ἐν ταῖς ἡμέραις ⌜Ἀντίπας⌝, ὁ
μάρτυς μου, ὁ πιστός [μου], ὃς ἀπεκτάνθη παρ' ὑμῖν,
14 ὅπου ὁ Σατανᾶς κατοικεῖ. ἀλλὰ ἔχω κατὰ σοῦ
⌜ὀλίγα, ὅτι⌝ ἔχεις ἐκεῖ κρατοῦντας τὴν διδαχὴν
Βαλαάμ, ὃς ἐδίδασκεν τῷ Βαλὰκ βαλεῖν σκάνδαλον
ἐνώπιον τῶν γιῶν Ἰϲραήλ, φαγεῖν εἰδωλόθυτα καὶ πορ-
15 νεῖϲαι· οὕτως ἔχεις καὶ σὺ κρατοῦντας τὴν διδαχὴν
16 Νικολαϊτῶν ὁμοίως. μετανόησον οὖν· εἰ δὲ μή,
ἔρχομαί σοι ταχύ, καὶ πολεμήσω μετ' αὐτῶν ἐν τῇ
17 ῥομφαίᾳ τοῦ στόματός μου. Ὁ ἔχων οὖς ἀκουσάτω
τί τὸ πνεῦμα λέγει ταῖς ἐκκλησίαις. Τῷ νικῶντι
δώϲω αὐτῷ τοῦ μάννα τοῦ κεκρυμμένου, καὶ δώϲω

13 †...†   14 ὀλίγα·

ship which was virtually a worship of
evil, and even as the symbol of wisdom
it is the wisdom that is ἐπίγειος ψυ-
χική, δαιμονιώδης, not that which comes
from above. Doubtless it is also the
venomous serpent, and the persecution told of its evil power.

κρατ. τ. ὄν. μου] refusing to abandon
it or be ashamed of it.

Reading somewhat difficult, also
construction: but unimportant. Probably Ἀντίπας undeclined, and then ὁ
μ. in nominative apposition (so Bleek).
Probably, as is said, contraction of
Ἀντίπατρος, a Macedonian and now
common name: but the contraction
seems to be unknown.

The phrase seems to shew that A.'s
death had happened some time ago.
Eus. iv. 16 fin. speaks of martyrdoms
of Carpus, Papylus, and Agathonice at
Pergamum in second century.

14. ἐδίδ. τῷ Βαλάκ] διδάσκω governs
a dat. twice in Plut. as well as in late
inferior writers.

βαλ. σκάνδ.] exactly the true sense
of σκ.

The words are from Num. xxxi. 16;
xxv. 1, 2.

Ἰσρ.] purposely put in (cf. 9) to mark
the Church as the true Israel.

For a similar reference to Balaam cf.
2 Pet. ii. 15; Jude 11; also (Plumptre)
1 Cor. x. 7, 8.

Plumptre is very good on εἰδωλόθ.
and πορν. The view of St Paul and
St John is essentially the same, though
the position different. Cf. 1 Cor. x.
14 φεύγετε ἀπὸ τ. εἰδωλολ.

15. The Nicolaitans must therefore have had something distinctly
analogous to the characteristics of
Balaam. They must have made use
of some kind of specious prophetic
teaching of a libertine type, as we see
was the case at Thyatira (20).

16. πολεμ....ῥομφ....στόμ.] cf. xix.
15, as well as v. 12 and i. 16.

17. τ. μάννα τ. κεκρ.] Ps. lxxviii.
(lxxvii.) 24. Here we come to the
third O.T. reminiscence, the days of
the Exodus.

τ. κεκρ.] probably in opposition to
the visible; hidden away in God's
treasures; very possibly with reference to the manna being hidden in
the ark of the covenant (mentioned
xi. 19), but not probably to the tradi-

αὐτῷ ψῆφον λευκήν, καὶ ἐπὶ τὴν ψῆφον ὄνομα καινόν
γεγραμμένον ὃ οὐδεὶς οἶδεν εἰ μὴ ὁ λαμβάνων.

Καὶ τῷ ἀγγέλῳ τῷ ἐν Θυατείροις ἐκκλησίας 18
γράψον

Τάδε λέγει ὁ υἱὸς τοῦ θεοῦ, ὁ ἔχων τογc ὀφθαλ-
μογc [αγτογ] ὡς φλόγα πυρός, καὶ οἱ πόδεc αγτογ ὅμοιοι
χαλκολιβάνῳ, Οἶδά σου τὰ ἔργα, καὶ τὴν ἀγάπην 19
καὶ τὴν πίστιν καὶ τὴν διακονίαν καὶ τὴν ὑπομονήν
σου, καὶ τὰ ἔργα σου τὰ ἔσχατα πλείονα τῶν
πρώτων. ἀλλὰ ἔχω κατὰ σοῦ ὅτι ἀφεῖς τὴν 20

tion of its being preserved by Jeremiah on Mount Pisgah (cf. 2 Mac. ii. 4).

The manna very likely opposed to the εἰδωλόθυτα, the fleshpots of Egypt, banquets. Cf. 1 Cor. viii. 10 ἐν εἰδωλίῳ κατακείμενον.

ὄν. καινόν] Is. lxii. 2; lxv. 15; cf. Apoc. iii. 12.

In the whole passage there seem to be allusions which we can only imperfectly trace to customs connected with the Asclepeum. Aristides i. 520 (304) says, " I am myself also one of those who have lived under the god, not two, but many and various lives, and who hold their disease to be profitable for this reason; and further καὶ ψήφους εἰληφότων, for which (ἀνθ' ὧν) I for my part would not exchange all that among men is called happiness." Also there seem to be various allusions to names given by Asclepius in dreams, e.g. i. 352 (627) οἱ δ' οὖν χρησμοὶ τοιοῦτοί τινες ἦσαν. ἐνεγέγραπτο μὲν τὸ ὄνομα τὸ ἐμὸν οὑτωσί, Αἴλιος Αριστείδης· καὶ σχεδὸν ἐκ διαλειμμάτων ἄλλα καὶ ἄλλα ἐπίσημα τ. ὀνόματος· προσενεγράψατο δὲ Σωσιμένης, καὶ ἕτερα τοιαῦτα σωτηρίαν ἐπαγγελλόμενα.

18. *Thyatira*. There is very little known about it. It is called by Ptolemy μητρόπολις. A large Turkish town now, and apparently large in ancient times. We learn from Epiph. li. 33, p. 455 AB that the Alogi cavilled at these words,

saying, οὐκ ἔνι ἐκεῖ ἐκκλησία Χριστιανῶν ἐν Θυατειροῖς· πῶς οὖν ἔγραφε τῇ μὴ οὔσῃ; This was probably in Hippolytus' time, early in the third century. It seems to imply that the church there had ceased to exist; but of this we know nothing.

ὁ υἱὸς τ. θεοῦ] This is singular coming in here rather than earlier, not having occurred in i., and not repeated later in the book. The Jewish Messianic name (from Ps. ii. 7; lxxxix. 26 f.) is probably the starting-point: but the coming of Christ and that which the Apostles had learned of its meaning, had given the name a deeper sense; cf. i. 6; ii. 28; iii. 5, 21; xiv. 1.

χαλκολιβ.] Near Sardis was a place for making electrum, doubtless from the gold dust, and Thyatira is in the same region.

19. διακον.] Cf. Mt. xx. 28 for verb: also for subst. in this wider sense, Eph. iv. 12; Heb. i. 14.

20. ἀφεῖς *sic*] Similarly iii. 9 διδῶ and xxii. 2 (probably) ἀποδιδοῦν, from ἀφέω and διδόω. We may consider ἀφίω and ἀφέω as parallel forms, the latter alone being contracted. It is a mistake to put the circumflex on ἀφιοῦσιν: no authority whatever for ἀφιέω, or any contract form including ι.

τ. γυν.] σου has some good ancient authority but seems to be an interpolation, so that we may drop this

⌜γυναῖκα⌝ Ἰεζάβελ, ἡ λέγουσα ἑαυτὴν προφῆτιν, καὶ
διδάσκει καὶ πλανᾷ τοὺς ἐμοὺς δούλους πορνεῦσαι καὶ
21 φαγεῖν εἰδωλόθυτα. καὶ ἔδωκα αὐτῇ χρόνον ἵνα μετα-
νοήσῃ, καὶ οὐ θέλει μετανοῆσαι ἐκ τῆς πορνείας
22 αὐτῆς. ἰδοὺ βάλλω αὐτὴν εἰς κλίνην, καὶ τοὺς μοι-
χεύοντας μετ᾽ αὐτῆς εἰς θλίψιν μεγάλην, ἐὰν μὴ
23 μετανοήσουσιν ἐκ τῶν ἔργων ⌜αὐτῆς⌝· καὶ τὰ τέκνα
αὐτῆς ἀποκτενῶ ἐν θανάτῳ· καὶ γνώσονται πᾶσαι αἱ

20 γυναῖκά σου   22 αὐτῶν

verse as having any bearing on the sense of ἄγγελος. If it did refer to a human ruler, the reference would be of a nature not applicable to the Church itself, and thus inconsistent with the general drift of these epistles.

Ἰεζάβελ] No one of this name known except the queen. Of course no Jew would bear it, so that if a real name it must have belonged to some Phoenician or kindred race. It is somewhat difficult to take it as a pseudonym referring to the original Jezebel, considering the different phrasing of 14 f., and the remoteness of a heathen queen from anything likely here : but on the whole this seems most likely. The chief allusion (Trench) is probably to Jehu's answer to Joram, 2 Ki. ix. 22, when her φάρμακα τὰ πολλά are mentioned with her whoredoms. Cf. the combination in Apoc. ix. 21 ; xxi. 8 ; xxii. 15 (in these last two coupled with idolatries). She was probably connected with the Nicolaitans. The Montanist prophetesses of Phrygia must not be forgotten.

Nothing can really be built on the inscription (CIG 3509) to which Blakesley refers recording how a man built a tomb in an unoccupied spot πρὸς τῷ Σαμβαθείῳ ἐν τῷ Χαλδαίου περιβόλῳ (cf. Periz. in Ael. V. H. 12. 35). Sambethe was the name of the Sibyl variously called Babylonian, Chaldaean, Jewish (Suid. s. v. Σίβυλλα; Schol. on Plat. Phaedr. p. 244):

another name being Sabba (Paus. x. 12. 9). The word Χαλδαίου makes an odd coincidence, but no tolerable explanation has been given.

The false prophetess stands opposed to the true prophetesses, as Hannah (Lk. ii. 36), Philip's daughters (Acts xxi. 9), and the prophetesses of Joel in Acts ii. 17 f. At Philippi (Acts xvi. 14—18) the conversion of Lydia, a purple-seller of Thyatira, is immediately followed by the incident of the ventriloquist damsel : but no connexion is marked between them.

False prophecy has an important place in the Apocalypse (xvi. 13 &c.), as in the N.T. generally. This was a common form of the revived heathenisms of the first, second and third centuries.

The teaching itself was probably of the adiaphoric kind: see v. 24.

22. κλίνην] may be only the bed of pain (Ps. xli. (xl.) 4), but more probably is the funeral bier or bed laid on a bier. This was one of the meanings of κλίνη, as of the Latin lectus, but in either case a reference is implied to the bed of pleasure.

23. τέκνα] Probably those who become her disciples (not= οἱ μοιχ.), and so reproduce her characteristics: cf. Is. lvii. 3.

θανάτῳ] stands evidently for דֶּבֶר, pestilence, which is nearly always (35 times) in LXX. θάνατος, also the Mod. Greek for pestilence. So Latin mor-

ἐκκλησίαι ὅτι ἐγώ εἰμι ὁ ἐραγνῶν νεφροὺς καὶ καρδίας,
καὶ δώσω ὑμῖν ἑκάστῳ κατὰ τὰ ἔργα ὑμῶν. ὑμῖν δὲ 24
λέγω τοῖς λοιποῖς τοῖς ἐν Θυατείροις, ὅσοι οὐκ
ἔχουσιν τὴν διδαχὴν ταύτην, οἵτινες οὐκ ἔγνωσαν τὰ
βαθέα τοῦ Σατανᾶ, ὡς λέγουσιν, οὐ βάλλω ἐφ' ὑμᾶς
ἄλλο βάρος· πλὴν ὃ ἔχετε κρατήσατε ἄχρι οὗ ἂν 25
ἥξω. Καὶ ὁ νικῶν καὶ ὁ τηρῶν ἄχρι τέλους τὰ ἔργα 26
μου, δώσω αὐτῷ ἐξουσίαν ἐπὶ τῶν ἐθνῶν, καὶ ποιμανεῖ 27
αὐτοὺς ἐν ῥάβδῳ σιδηρᾷ ὡς τὰ σκεύη τὰ κεραμικὰ συντρί-

---

talitas. Cf. vi. 8; (xviii. 8). As a
Hebrew reduplication, there would be
neither force nor grammar.

ἐραυν. νεφ. &c.] He is not one
who shews a promiscuous favour to
Christians as such, but a searching
trial of (1) inward and (2) outward
morality. The reins mainly answer
to the emotions, the heart to what
we should call the mind. From Ps.
vii. 10; xxvi. (xxv.) 2; xxviii. (xxvii.)
4; lxii. (lxi.) 13; Jer. xvii. 10.

24. *τὰ βαθέα τ. Σατ.*] cf. 1 Cor. ii.
10 τ. θεοῦ. Of later Gnostics we read
that they professed alone to know τὰ
βάθη, which may or may not refer to
St Paul. It was in any case a natural
phrase (τ.β. alone) for men who claimed
an esoteric knowledge, which was sure
in some cases to mean a superiority to
morality, a "Higher Law." A deli-
berate libertinism, founded on con-
tempt of the body, or antagonism to
the creator power or powers, or complete experience, was certainly found
in some inferior Gnostic schools (by
no means the greatest), as the Cainites
and Carpocratians. But how far back
the roots of the doctrine go, we do
not know. Here τ. Σατ. taken with
ὁ θρ. τ. Σατ. suggest depths connected
with Ophitic worship.

ὡς λέγ.] may go either with what
goes before, though it can hardly be
literally true as regards τ. Σατ. or
better perhaps with what follows,
meaning that these teachers professed

the deliverance from superfluous bur-
dens.

βάρος] A curious coincidence with
Acts xv. 28, but probably accidental.

25. *κρατήσατε*] not as we might
expect *κρατεῖτε.* Once for all take a
firm hold upon what you have been
taught: make it a real power, not a
tradition.

26. *καὶ ὁ νικῶν*] In this the first
epistle in which Ὁ οὖς is placed last,
the promise is directly connected with
what precedes (Ewald).

26 f. The promise is taken from the
conquest of Canaan; the words from
Ps. ii. 8 f. *ποιμανεῖ* of LXX. answers
to Masor. םֵעֹרְתּ from עַעָר, to break
(so Job xxxiv. 24 Heb.), differing only
by a letter from הָעָר, for which *ποι-
μαίνω* is the common LXX. rendering.
The Greek phrase is amply justified in
O.T. usage by Mic. v. 6; cf. vii. 14 as
to phrase. The *ῥάβδος*, טֶבֵשׁ, a tribe,
sceptre &c. represents authority rather
than violence and is used Ps. xxiii. 4,
cf. Lev. xxvii. 32, for the shepherd's
implement. It is by no means impossible that the LXX. reading is the true
one in the Psalm (Jerome's Hebrew
version only turns *reges* of the Roman
and Gallican Psalters into *pasces*): if
not, it is a striking adaptation. The
Lord is the shepherd of all the nations
even in His utmost severity. Cf. xii.
5; xix. 15.

27. *ὡς τὰ σκεύη* &c.] More difficult
with *ποιμανεῖ.* But probably an idea

28 Βεται, ὡς κἀγὼ εἴληφα παρὰ τοῦ πατρός μου, καὶ
29 δώσω αὐτῷ τὸν ἀστέρα τὸν πρωινόν. Ὁ ἔχων οὖς
   ἀκουσάτω τί τὸ πνεῦμα λέγει ταῖς ἐκκλησίαις.

III. 1   Καὶ τῷ ἀγγέλῳ ⌈τῆς⌉ ἐν Σάρδεσιν ἐκκλησίας
          γράψον
          Τάδε λέγει ὁ ἔχων τὰ ἑπτὰ πνεύματα τοῦ θεοῦ
          καὶ τοὺς ἑπτὰ ἀστέρας Οἶδά σου τὰ ἔργα, ὅτι
      2 ὄνομα ἔχεις ὅτι ζῆς, καὶ νεκρὸς εἶ. γίνου γρηγορῶν,
          καὶ στήρισον τὰ λοιπὰ ἃ ἔμελλον ἀποθανεῖν, οὐ γὰρ

                              1 †τῷ†

of remaking, as Jer. xviii. 2—10. In
Jer. xix. 11 the judicial breaking is
mentioned alone.

ὡς κἀγὼ εἴληφα]. Cf. Mt. xxviii. 18.
28. τ. ἀστ. τ. πρω.] (in xii. 16
Christ is himself ὁ ἀστ. ὁ λαμπ. ὁ πρω.)
it can hardly refer to the righteous
shining as the sun, in Dan. or Mt.
δώσω implies something more. The
Star must here be one ensign of
royalty, as the ῥάβδος was another.
They are combined in Balaam's prophecy, Num. xxiv. 17, cf. Is. xiv. 12
(on which see Delitzsch and Gesenius,
who quotes the Arab. Kamus, "the star
of a people" for the prince; and shews
that in Chald. and Arab. the Morning
Star was preeminently called the
Bright Star) and Bar-cochab. Our
Lord Himself *is* the Star, as He is
the ῥίζα and γένος of David, not
merely the Son of David; but others
share His rule (as here) and so receive
the Star. Doubtless not rule only is
meant, but light, and dawning light:
cf. Lk. i. 78 f.; ii. 32.

The special force for Thyatira is
unknown. Probably something local
was concerned in a staff or sceptre
and a star.

III. 1. *Sardes:* the famous capital
of Lydia.

ὁ ἔχ. τὰ ἑ. πνεύμ.] See i. 4; iv. 5;
v. 6, which last explains ὁ ἔχων; v. 6
being itself founded on Zech. iv. 10.
There as here the Spirits belong to

the Son, which is not indicated in
i. 4. These variations shew that we
are dealing with images, no one of
which sets forth the complete truth.
The intermediate passage is iv. 5, the
seven blazing lights of which are
probably referred to here with the
seven stars.

ὄν. ἔχ. ὅτι] Düst. after Wolf cites
Herod. vii. 138, ἡ στρατηλασίη...οὔνομα
μὲν εἶχε ὡς ἐπ' Ἀθήνας ἐλαύνει, κατίετο
δὲ ἐς πᾶσαν τ. Ἑλλάδα. The theory
of a Bishop *Zosimus* is most unlikely,
though paronomasiæ do occur in N.T.

2. γίνου γρ.] shew thyself, not
'become,' any more than in ii. 10
which would be γένου.

ἔμελλον] (not μέλλει, which is another invention of Eras., the whole
clause being absent from his MS.).
They were in this state when the
great crisis came.

τὰ λοιπά] usually taken as 'surviving,'
as if καταλοιπά, ὑπολοιπά. The sense
suits the context, but I can find no
authority. The Latins have *cetera,*
which is the proper sense, and so
apparently Andr. and Areth., rather
confusedly, as if τὰ λοιπά are the
other μέλη of the angel, dying only
as opposed to those already dead.
Xenophon and Plato use τὰ λοιπά
half adverbially for things future as
opposed to the past; and this makes
good sense; but the order shews that
τὰ λ. must be governed by στήρ. and

εὕρηκά σου ᵀ ἔργα πεπληρωμένα ἐνώπιον τοῦ θεοῦ
μου· μνημόνευε οὖν πῶς εἴληφας καὶ ἤκουσας καὶ 3
τήρει, καὶ μετανόησον· ἐὰν οὖν μὴ γρηγορήσῃς, ἥξω
ὡς κλέπτης, καὶ οὐ μὴ ⌐γνῷς⌐ ποίαν ὥραν ἥξω ἐπὶ
σέ· ἀλλὰ ἔχεις ὀλίγα ὀνόματα ἐν Σάρδεσιν ἃ οὐκ 4
ἐμόλυναν τὰ ἱμάτια αὐτῶν, καὶ περιπατήσουσιν μετ᾽
ἐμοῦ ἐν λευκοῖς, ὅτι ἄξιοί εἰσιν. Ὁ νικῶν οὕτως 5
περιβαλεῖται ἐν ἱματίοις λευκοῖς, καὶ οὐ μὴ ἐξαλείψω

2 τὰ　　　　　　　　　　3 γνώσῃ

be antecedent to ἅ. But on the whole
it is best to take it in the accepted
sense, as a kind of Hebraism אֲשֶׁר
and שְׁאֵרִית, both of which often mean
a remnant, but are also sometimes
rendered by λοιπός. In like manner
we have λίμμα beside κατάλιμμα and
ὑπόλιμμα.

ἔργα] probably without τά, "found
no works of thine fulfilled."

πεπληρ.] brought to their right and
natural fulfilment)(left in a per-
functory maimed state.

ἐνώπ.] i.e. by a conventional standard
they might be called πεπληρ.: but not
before God.

3. εἴληφας] On comparison with
v. 7; viii. 5; xi. 17, (ii. 27 neutral)
it seems probable that εἴληφα is used
in Apoc. as an aorist. So apparently
εἴρηκα vii. 14; xix. 3; and perhaps
elsewhere as Heb. x. 9; 2 Cor. xii. 9.
λαμβάνω is not to be confounded with
δέχομαι. Not welcome, but simply
(neutral) reception. Cf. 1 Th. i. 5 ff.;
ii. 1 ff.; 1 Cor. ii. 1 &c.

ὡς κλέπτης] from Mt. xxiv. 43 ||.

ποίαν] as Mt. xxiv. 42 f. not dis-
tinguishable from τίνα.

ποίαν ὥραν] Perhaps only an attraction. But it is curious that Jn. iv. 52
has ἐχθὲς ὥραν ἑβδόμην ἀφῆκεν αὐτὸν ὁ
πυρετός. So Passio Pauli vi. (Cod.
Patm.) ὥραν ἐννάτην ἑστώτων πολλῶν.
Cyr. Hier. has ἐσταυρώθη τρίτην ὥραν
(Catech. xiii. 24). Alford has entirely
misunderstood Krüger and Matthæi,
who speak only of repeated action with

ordinals (Jn. iv. 52 ordinal, but not
repeated: this is neither). Acts x. 3
wrongly cited by Winer &c., for the
better MSS. insert περί. [Yet see Acts
x. 30.]

ἥξω] arrive.

4. ὀνόματα] cf. xi. 13; also Acts
i. 15. Probably the distinct personality
is intended.

οὐκ ἐμόλ. τὰ ἱμ.])(πλύνω, of vii. 14;
xxii. 14. This is negative: their
natural garments remain undefiled:
the other is positive, they have changed
their natural colour to white. Their
manner of life seems intended. In
Jude 23 (apparently from Zech. iii.
3 f.) the conception is different.

περιπατ. μετ᾽ ἐμοῦ] Not the ethical
or religious walking with God of
Enoch or Noah (Gen. v. 22; vi. 9:
cf. Mic. vi. 8; Mal. ii. 6); but the
converse of God's walking with men
(ii. 1): see also the language of 2 Sam.
vii. 6 f. (|| Chr.): "that where I am,
ye may be also" (Jn. xvii. 24): yet
not merely presence with Christ, but
association in His activities is described as walking.

5. The best authorities are unanimous for οὕτως: otherwise οὗτος
differing only by itacism is not unlikely.
οὕτως may either be inferential (as
possibly iii. 16) or like ὡσαύτως, which
seems on the whole simplest.

λευκοῖς] the colour of sanctity. So
in the Transfiguration &c.

ἐξαλ....βίβ. τ. ζω.] Ex. xxxii. 33;
Ps. lxix, (lxviii.) 28.

τὸ ὄνομα αὐτοῦ ἐκ τῆϲ Βίβλογ τῆϲ ζωῆϲ, καὶ ὁμολο-
γήσω τὸ ὄνομα αὐτοῦ ἐνώπιον τοῦ πατρός μου καὶ
6 ἐνώπιον τῶν ἀγγέλων αὐτοῦ. Ὁ ἔχων οὖς ἀκουσάτω
τί τὸ πνεῦμα λέγει ταῖς ἐκκλησίαις.

7 Καὶ τῷ ἀγγέλῳ ⌐τῆς⌐ ἐν Φιλαδελφίᾳ ἐκκλησίας
γράψον

Τάδε λέγει ⌐ὁ ἅγιος, ὁ ἀληθινός⌐, ὁ ἔχων τὴν
κλεῖν ⌐ Δαγείδ, ὁ ἀνοίγων καὶ ογδεὶϲ κλείϲει, καὶ ⌐κλείων⌐
8 καὶ ογδεὶϲ ἀνοίγει, Οἶδά σου τὰ ἔργα,– ἰδοὺ δέδωκα
ἐνώπιόν σου θύραν ἠνεῳγμένην, ἣν οὐδεὶς δύναται
κλεῖσαι αὐτήν,– ὅτι μικρὰν ἔχεις δύναμιν, καὶ

7 †τῷ† | ὁ ἀληθινός, ὁ ἅγιος | τοῦ | κλείει

τ. πατ....τ. ἀγγ.] combines Mt. x. 32
with Lk. xii. 8.

The whole promise seems to refer
to membership of the holy people in
the holy land. On βίβ. ζωῆς see
Plumptre and Ewald; Is. iv. 3; Ezek.
xiii. 9; Ps. lxxxvii. *passim*.

7. *Philadelphia:* little known, one
of Ignatius' letters addressed to it.

ὁ ἅγ. ὁ ἀληθ.] best interpreted by
vi. 10, where the souls of the martyrs
cry, "How long, O Master, ὁ ἅγ. ὁ
ἀληθ., dost thou not judge and avenge
our blood &c.?" As holy, He is of
purer eyes, than to behold iniquity,
He must be the avenger of these
hideous crimes on earth; as true, He
must fulfil His word and His attributes, not forsaking His servants or
leaving His law unvindicated. Christ
was recognised by the demons as the
Holy One of God, the pure and perfect
expression of the heavenly holiness
(Mk. i. 24; Lk. iv. 34); and it was in
this form that Peter confessed Him
(John vi. 69 true reading: cf. Acts
iii. 14).

For ἀληθινός it is misleading to
think only of the classical sense, true
as *genuine* (True and Living God)(
vain and dead εἴδωλα). Not only vi. 10
(just cited) but iii. 14 ὁ μάρτυς ὁ

πιστὸς καὶ [ὁ] ἀληθινός (cf. xix. 11),
and what is said of His "ways" or
"judgments" (xv. 3; xvi. 7; xix. 2),
ἀληθ. coupled with δίκαιος, shew that
the Apoc. retains the O.T. conception
of truth, expressed e.g. in Ps. cxlvi. 6
"which keepeth truth for ever," i.e.
constancy to a plighted word or purpose, the opposite of caprice. In LXX.
ἀληθής is never personal, while ἀληθινός
is so used a little, of God Ex. xxxiv. 6;
Is. lxv. 16; Ps. lxxxvi. 15; of men
Job ii. 3; viii. 6 (ἀλήθεια in the
corresponding sense very common,
especially in Psalms); also Gr. Esr. viii.
89; 3 Mac. ii. 11 (with πιστός).

κλεῖν &c.] of course from Eliakim,
Is. xxii. 15 ff. (cf. i. 18; Mt. xvi. 19).
Conceivably suggested by the κλειδοῦ-
χοι (sc. of "a sanctuary")—priestesses,
who carried a key adorned with wool
as a symbol. As the Davidean king,
at once Son of David and Root of
David, He holds the key of the city
of David, the new Jerusalem (*v.* 12).
His opening is doubtless primarily
the admission of the Gentiles despite
Jewish resistance. His shutting is
the exclusion of unbelieving Israel
despite their parentage and privileges.

8. ἰδού...κλεῖσαι αὐτήν] a parenthesis. It expresses what was partly

ἐτήρησάς μου τὸν λόγον, καὶ οὐκ ἠρνήσω τὸ ὄνομά
μου. ἰδοὺ διδῶ ἐκ τῆς συναγωγῆς τοῦ Σατανᾶ, τῶν 9
λεγόντων ἑαυτοὺς Ἰουδαίους εἶναι, καὶ οὐκ εἰσὶν ἀλλὰ
ψεύδονται, – ἰδοὺ ποιήσω αὐτοὺς ἵνα ΗΞΟΥϹΙΝ ΚΑῚ
ΠΡΟϹΚΥΝΗϹΟΥϹΙΝ ΕΝΏΠΙΟΝ ΤῶΝ ΠΟΔῶΝ ϹΟΥ, καὶ γνῶσιν
ὅτι ἐγὼ ΗΓΆΠΗϹΆ ϹΕ. ὅτι ἐτήρησας τὸν λόγον τῆς 10
ὑπομονῆς μου, κἀγώ σε τηρήσω ἐκ τῆς ὥρας τοῦ
πειρασμοῦ τῆς μελλούσης ἔρχεσθαι ἐπὶ τῆς οἰκου-
μένης ὅλης, πειράσαι τοὺς κατοικοῦντας ἐπὶ τῆς γῆς.
ἔρχομαι ταχύ· κράτει ὃ ἔχεις, ἵνα μηδεὶς λάβῃ τὸν 11
στέφανόν σου. Ὁ νικῶν ποιήσω αὐτὸν στύλον ἐν 12

identical with their works, partly a fruit of it. The reality and activity of their faith had by God's gift brought them to have before them an opened door, i.e. doubtless a favourable opportunity for gaining access and influence within the surrounding population (cf. 1 Co. xvi. 9; 2 Co. ii. 12; Col. iv. 3). Looked at from the other side, the door would also be for the entrance of converts into the Christian fold (cf. Acts xiv. 27). Οἶδά σου τὰ ἔργα...ὅτι as usual.

μικ. ἔχ. δύν.] The Philadelphian Christian community was small and weak, and doubtless unsustained by the help of including in its number rich or influential citizens. Yet it had kept Christ's word, and not denied His name.

Even unbelieving Jews were to be given as new members to the Philadelphian Church.

9. διδῶ] (taken Hebraically) might be only the vague "make": but the notion seems rather "I give men of &c., as thy converts": cf. what follows. In any case the sentence is broken.

ἤξ. &c.] St John here borrows the old prophetic language written for the Gentiles. Is. xlv. 14; lx. 14; lxvi. 23 context.

ἐγὼ ἠγάπ.] Is. xliii. 4 context.

They shall take the place of heathen, and acknowledge thee as the true Israel.

10. "The word of my endurance," a marvellously compressed phrase, by which the simple μου τ. λόγον of v. 8 is made more definite. To embrace and hold fast the gospel of the Crucified was to embrace and hold fast the Gospel of Christ's own endurance, at once as an example and as a power.

ὥρας] the appointed special time: cf. xiv. 7, 15.

πειρασμοῦ] trial in the strictest sense; not simply affliction (as Dr Hatch has recently tried to shew), but affliction as probation, exactly as the next clause explains, πειράσαι τ. κατοικ. ἐ. τ. γῆς. This combination is itself remarkable; for οἱ κατοικ. ἐ. τ. γῆς (apparently from Hos. iv. 1) occurs in ten other places of Apoc., and always in a bad sense. "The men given up to evil and to hatred of God's saints." Yet to them too the calamities will be not retribution only but also trial, if perchance one here or there may thereby be brought to a better mind.

οἰκουμένης] the civilised world, the empire.

11. λάβῃ τ. στέφ.] Cf. Col. ii. 18 καταβραβ.; also 2 Ti. ii. 5.

τῷ ναῷ τοῦ θεοῦ μου, καὶ ἔξω οὐ μὴ ἐξέλθῃ ἔτι, καὶ
γράψω ἐπ' αὐτὸν τὸ ὄνομα τοῦ θεοῦ μου καὶ τὸ
ὄνομα τῆϲ πόλεωϲ τοῦ θεοῦ μου, τῆς καινῆς Ἰερουσα-
λήμ, ἡ καταβαίνουσα ἐκ τοῦ οὐρανοῦ ἀπὸ τοῦ θεοῦ
13 μου, καὶ τὸ ὄνομά μου τὸ καινόν. Ὁ ἔχων οὖς
ἀκουσάτω τί τὸ πνεῦμα λέγει ταῖς ἐκκλησίαις.

14 Καὶ τῷ ἀγγέλῳ ⌜τῆς⌝ ἐν Λαοδικίᾳ ἐκκλησίας
γράψον

Τάδε λέγει ὁ Ἀμήν, ὁ μάρτυϲ ὁ πιϲτὸϲ καὶ [ὁ]
15 ἀληθινός, ἡ ἀρχὴ τῆϲ κτίϲεωϲ τοῦ θεοῦ, Οἶδά σου τὰ
ἔργα, ὅτι οὔτε ψυχρὸς εἶ οὔτε ζεστός. ὄφελον
16 ψυχρὸς ἦς ἢ ζεστός. οὕτως, ὅτι χλιαρὸς εἶ καὶ
οὔτε ζεστὸς οὔτε ψυχρός, μέλλω σε ἐμέσαι ἐκ τοῦ
17 στόματός μου. ὅτι λέγεις ὅτι Πλούσιός εἰμι καὶ
πεπλούτηκα καὶ οὐδὲν χρείαν ἔχω, καὶ οὐκ οἶδας ὅτι
σὺ εἶ ὁ ταλαίπωρος καὶ ᵀ ἐλεινὸς καὶ πτωχὸς καὶ
18 τυφλὸς καὶ γυμνός, συμβουλεύω σοι ἀγοράσαι παρ'
ἐμοῦ χρυσίον πεπυρωμένον ἐκ πυρὸς ἵνα πλουτήσῃς,
καὶ ἱμάτια λευκὰ ἵνα περιβάλῃ καὶ μὴ φανερωθῇ ἡ
αἰσχύνη τῆϲ γυμνότητός σου, καὶ κολλούριον ἐγχρῖσαι
19 τοὺς ὀφθαλμούς σου ἵνα βλέπῃς. ἐγὼ ὅϲουϲ ἐὰν φιλῶ

14 †...†   17 ὁ

12. τὸ ὄν. τ. πό.] Ezek. xlviii. 35 (cf.
ii. 17).

τ. καιν.] (as ii. 17) Is. lxii. 2; lxv. 15.
The promise is of the temple and the
city, the kingly period, David and
Solomon.

14. Ἀμήν] Perhaps derived from
Is. lxv. 16 בֵּאלֹהֵי אָמֵן &c., at all
events the sure unchangeableness in
word and in work, the witnessing in
heaven of which the witnessing on
earth had been the signal manifestation.

ἡ ἀρχ. τ. κτίσ.] Prov. viii. 22, κύριος
ἔκτισέ με ἀρχὴν ὁδῶν αὐτοῦ εἰς ἔργα
αὐτοῦ, קָנָנִי רֵאשִׁית. The words do
not define the precise sense. On
ἀρχή as a term cf. Col. i. 18, and
for the probable idea Col. i. 16. The
words might no doubt bear the Arian
meaning "the first thing created":
but they equally well bear the sense
which the other Christological language of the book suggests, the being
antecedent to all creation, in whom
all creation came and comes to pass.
Christ's last testimony and His earliest
function seem purposely combined.

17. Hos. xii. 8.

ὁ ταλαίπ.] "for the very reason that
thou deemest thyself rich."

19. Prov. iii. 12, B has ἐλέγχει,

ἐλέγχω καὶ παιδεύω· ζήλευε οὖν καὶ μετανόησον. Ἰδοὺ 20
ἕστηκα ἐπὶ τὴν θύραν καὶ κρούω· ἐάν τις ἀκούσῃ τῆς
φωνῆς μου καὶ ἀνοίξῃ τὴν θύραν, ᵀ εἰσελεύσομαι πρὸς
αὐτὸν καὶ δειπνήσω μετ᾽ αὐτοῦ καὶ αὐτὸς μετ᾽ ἐμοῦ.
Ὁ νικῶν δώσω αὐτῷ καθίσαι μετ᾽ ἐμοῦ ἐν τῷ θρόνῳ 21
μου, ὡς κἀγὼ ἐνίκησα καὶ ἐκάθισα μετὰ τοῦ πατρός
μου ἐν τῷ θρόνῳ αὐτοῦ. Ὁ ἔχων οὖς ἀκουσάτω τί 22
τὸ πνεῦμα λέγει ταῖς ἐκκλησίαις.

20 καί

A &c. παιδεύει, παιδείας occurs in all
authorities in v. 11. In iv. 5 βρονταί and
φωναί seem also duplicate readings.

ζήλευε] ⟩(χλιαρός of 16.

20. Plumptre is certainly right as
to the general sense. Our Lord as a
guest in the Gospels supplies the
foundation. He knocks asking to be
admitted into the household and festival (cf. Cana) as One whose presence
is right there. Then αὐτὸς μετ᾽ αὐτοῦ
(with reference to the marriage supper

of the Lamb) follows as it were inci-
dentally.

21. ἐνίκησα] as before.

ἐκάθισα] The image from Ps. cx. 1.
Several times in N.T. as Mt. xxvi. 64 |||;
[Mk.] xvi. 19; Acts ii. 30, 34; Eph.
i. 20; Col. iii. 1; Heb. i. 13.

This last promise gathers up the
crowning event of Israel's history, the
Resurrection and Ascension of the
King.

Note on the text of II. 1 etc.

It will be observed that the inscription, mentioning the temple of the Augusti at Ephesus as the recipient of the gift of the Macedonian Hyrcani, has no article before ναῷ, and that although τῷ ἐν Ἐφέσῳ follows. The same usage prevails universally, as far as I have seen, in the many inscriptions from the province of Asia which describe persons as priests or priestesses of the temple (temples) of Asia in this or that principal city. One inscription at Smyrna (*C. I. G.* 3266) sets forth a fine as to be paid in a certain contingency τοῖς ἐν Σμύρνῃ ναοῖς τῶν Σεβαστῶν : and this not quite pertinent exception may prove to be not as solitary as it now appears. But at least in the current personal designation, of which sufficient examples will be found in Marquardt's and Waddington's notes, the article, inserted after ναοῦ or ναῶν, is omitted before it, the formula being ἀρχιερεὺς [τῆς] Ἀσίας ναοῦ τοῦ (ναῶν τῶν) ἐν Ἐφέσῳ.

Now there is much reason to believe that a similar grammatical peculiarity distinguishes the headings of St John's letters to the 'angels' of the Seven Churches of Asia. It does not appear in the text adopted by Tischendorf from the bulk of MSS., which runs Καὶ τῷ ἀγγέλῳ τῆς ἐν Ἐφέσῳ (Σμύρνῃ κ.τ.λ.) ἐκκλησίας γράψον, nor in the adjectival modifications inherited by the Received Text from Erasmus in three cases (τῆς Ἐφεσίνης ἐκκλησίας, τῆς ἐκκλησίας Σμυρναίων, τῆς ἐκκλησίας Λαοδικέων). But A and C replace τῆς by τῷ for Ephesus (reading Καὶ τῷ ἀγγέλῳ τῷ ἐν Ἐφέσῳ ἐκκλησίας), and A for Smyrna and Thyatira, in which last case C drops the article. Griesbach gives τῷ a place in his margin for Ephesus; Tregelles goes a step further by exchanging text and margin; Lachmann follows A in all three cases, and no editor could safely do more as regards the text itself. But τῷ can hardly be wrong when it is thus attested, and it is difficult to believe that it was not the original reading in the four other places.

In the paucity of primary authorities for the text of the Apocalypse a numerically very small amount of authority must inevitably be accepted in some of the cases where they differ from each other. In this book A and C approve themselves as standing clearly above other MSS. They are both often wrong singly: but the morally certain readings in which A stands nearly or even quite alone are likewise not few; and when both agree, they carry peculiar weight. ℵ abounds both in vulgar corruptions and in paraphrastic changes of its own, though it has a large good element. The right deviations of P from the commoner texts are but scattered, and in Q they are still rarer. Thus the dissent of three out of the five uncials is not a serious difficulty. The best cursive of the Apocalypse is, I think, 95, the Parham MS. collated by Dr Scrivener; and it omits ἐκκλησίας for Laodicea and apparently for Smyrna, in which place it certainly puts ὁ for τῇ. This omission is readily explained if a text with τῷ for τῆς preceded, but otherwise is unaccountable: nor can it be accidental, for even A has it for Thyatira, the Syriac for Sardis, and the first hand of the Amiatine MS. of the Latin Vulgate for Ephesus. A second good cursive, 36, has τῷ ἀγγέλῳ τῷ τῆς Ἐφέσῳ ἐκκλησίας (so Alter prints, ii. 943). Another Greek trace of the reading occurs in two rough quotations by Epiphanius (455 B, D), γράψον τῷ ἀγγέλῳ τῆς ἐκκλησίας τῷ ἐν Θυατείροις, γράψον τῷ ἀγγέλῳ τῷ τῆς ἐν Θυατείροις ἐκκλησίας, which alike in different ways attest and soften off the difficulty of τῷ ἐν Θυατείροις ἐκκλησίας: it is tolerably certain that throughout the passage Epiphanius is copying Hippolytus (Lipsius *Zur Quellenkritik d. Epiphanios* 234; *Quellen d. ältesten Ketzergeschichte* 109 ff.), his predecessor by some 150 years. Nor is Latin evidence wanting. Tertullian barely alludes to these verses, and Cyprian does not touch them. But the large quotations of Cyprian in other parts of the Apocalypse enable us to see that his text is approximately represented by that of Primasius, although three centuries lie between them. Now in the text of Primasius *ecclesiae* precedes the name in the cases of Ephesus, Smyrna, Pergamum, and Laodicea, with the accession of Augustine for Ephesus, Jerome's translation of Origen for Pergamum (but *Ephesiorum ecclesiae*), and the Fulda MS. for Laodicea; while the same order survives in the Vulgate generally for Sardis : the transposition, it can hardly be doubted, is interpretative of τῷ, as in the first quotation by Epiphanius or Hippolytus. But further, in the three remaining cases no inference is needed to prove the presence of τῷ, for we find *angelo ecclesiae qui est Thyatirae* (*Sardis, Philadelphiae*). It seems probable that the Old Latin MS. used by Primasius had merely *ecclesiae* before the names of all the seven churches, and that *qui est* was inserted by

himself when it occurred to him to do so, that is, in three con-
secutive cases. His commentary shews various marks of independent
Greek criticism: and at the outset (Ephesus) an explanatory
remark of his, overlooked by editors of the New Testament, shews
beyond question, though not too clearly worded, that he had before
him a Greek MS. in which a τῷ followed ἀγγέλῳ. "Dativo hic casu
angelo posuit, non genetivo, (ac si diceret *Scribe angelo huic ecclesiae*,)
ut non tam angelum et ecclesiam separatim videatur dixisse quam
quis angelus exponere voluisset, unam scilicet faciens angeli ecclesiaeque personam." The evidence may be tabulated as follows:

ii	1	Ephesus AC (36) Prim^com.dis. Cf. Prim^txt Aug.
	8	Smyrna A. Cf. 95 am* : item Prim.
	12	Pergamum. Cf. Prim^txt Or.Hier.
	18	Thyatira A (om. ἐκκλησίας) Prim (Epiph = Hipp.). Cf. C.
iii	1	Sardis Prim. Cf. syr : item lat.vg.
	7	Philadelphia Prim.
	14	Laodicea. Cf. 95 : item fu Prim.

Extract from an article by J. Bovon, 'L'Hypothèse de M. Vischer Sur l'Origine de l'Apocalypse,' Revue de Théologie et de Philosophie, Lausanne, 1887.

"Τούτων δὲ οὕτως ἐχόντων écrit Irénée au sujet de chiffre de la bête 666 (Apoc. xiii. 18) καὶ ἐν πᾶσι τοῖς σπουδαίοις καὶ ἀρχαίοις ἀντιγράφοις τοῦ ἀριθμοῦ τούτου κειμένου, καὶ μαρτυρούντων αὐτῶν ἐκείνων τῶν κατ' ὄψιν τὸν Ἰωάννην ἑωρακότων.... Et un peu plus loin, toujours sur le même sujet : ἡμεῖς οὖν οὐκ ἀποκινδυνεύομεν περὶ τοῦ ὀνόματος τοῦ Ἀντιχρίστου ἀποφαινόμενοι βεβαιωτικῶς. Εἰ γὰρ ἔδει ἀναφανδὸν τῷ νῦν καιρῷ κηρύττεσθαι τοὔνομα αὐτοῦ, δι' ἐκείνου ἂν ἐρρέθη τοῦ καὶ τὴν Ἀποκάλυψιν ἑωρακότος. Οὐδὲ γὰρ πρὸ πολλοῦ χρόνου ἑωράθη, ἀλλὰ σχεδὸν ἐπὶ τῆς ἡμετέρας γενεᾶς πρὸς τῷ τέλει τῆς Δομετιανοῦ ἀρχῆς.

"On le voit, dans cette question de date, toute la discussion porte sur l'explication de l'aoriste ἑωράθη du second fragment. Le sujet de ce temps n'étant pas énoncé, il faut le sous-entendre ; or la proximité du participe ἑωρακότος (phrase précédente) semble indiquer que l'auteur pense encore à l'Apocalypse, qui 'aurait été vue' vers le fin du principat de Domitian, et c'est bien ainsi qu'a interprété l'ancienne Eglise. Seulement ce sens se heurte, me paraît-il, contre une double difficulté. (a) Si l'on consulte l'ensemble de la péricope, on reconnaîtra qu'Irénée n'avait pas à rappeler ici quand l'*Apocalypse* a été vue, mais jusqu'à quand l'*apôtre Jean* a vécu. La marche de la pensée est, en effet, la suivante. Irénée fait remarquer que, sur cette question de la signification du chiffre, il convient de s'exprimer avec réserve ; car, dit-il, si l'interprétation avait dû en être donnée, elle l'aurait été tout naturellement par celui qui a vu l'Apocalypse et qui a vécu presque jusqu'à nos jours. La Révélation, Irénée le reconnaît, n'explique pas ce symbole ; peu importait donc, en cette matière, la date de cet écrit. Mais ce qui importait, au contraire, c'est que celui qui seul aurait pu donner la clef de l'énigme, l'auteur du livre lui-même, vivait encore vers la fin du Ier siècle. Si donc il s'était expliqué sur ce point—telle paraît être l'idée d'Irénée,—nous n'aurions pas manqué de le savoir ; et le fait qu'il s'en est abstenu doit nous exhorter à la prudence.—Il me paraît donc plus naturel, vu le sens de la phrase, de sous-entendre[1] ὁ Ἰωάννης, et non ἡ

---

[1] Les défenseurs de cette idée ont fait remarquer que l'expression "avoir vu Jean" dans le sens de "avoir connu Jean" est familière à Irénée.

'Αποκάλυψις comme sujet de l'aor. ἐωράθη. Il y a là, sans doute, une certaine négligence de style; mais des incorrections de ce genre ne sont pas rares dans les écrits des anciens docteurs. (*b*) Ce qui confirmerait cette explication, c'est que le traducteur latin d'Irénée a rendu ἐωράθη, non par *visa est*, ce qui eût été de rigueur, s'il avait sous-entendu comme sujet 'l'Apocalypse'; mais par *visum est* (τὸ θηρίον). Puisqu'il s'est cru autorisé à changer le sujet, pourquoi la même liberté ne serait-elle pas accordée à la critique? En résumé, dans cette question de date, le témoignage qu'on invoque est trop incertain pour conduire à un résultat qui puisse être considéré comme vraiment acquis."

Dr Hort gave in lecture an analysis of the first of M. Bovon's arguments, admitting the difficulty of accounting for γὰρ on the common interpretation, and the force of the argument from the use of ὁράω with persons in Irenaeus.

He made no reference to the second argument. He called attention, however, to the fact that Irenaeus elsewhere (II. 22. 5; III. 3. 4) brings St John's life down to the times of Trajan.

GREEK INDEX.

ENGLISH INDEX.

HEBREW INDEX.

www.ingramcontent.com/pod-product-compliance
Lightning Source LLC
Chambersburg PA
CBHW071103090426
42737CB00013B/2455